EMBRACE THE UNKNOWN
THE JOURNALS OF STARDRAGON
A COLLECTION OF WISDOM, STORIES AND ESSAYS

Stardragon
___

A little about myself, I put together a collection of writings I have done through the years, instead of making a bunch of different books.

I was born in Milford, Mass in 1952, my parents named me Barbara Jean Ruggles. The name Jean is not a middle name, its suppose to be Barbara Jean.

I grew up in Franklin, Mass. went to the little red brick school house, and public schools. Then to Dean Jr. College one year, majored in math and science and took some other courses over time. I did not graduate from Dean. Instead I got married and life went on.

I have done all sorts of work in my life, from raising worms, to being a waitress in a oriental restaurant, from being a baker and selling home baked goods, a nurses aide, and taking in rescued animals and raising birds that fell out of their nests. Some even learned to talk! And now for the last 22 years running my own book business.

I have also raised three children, one grandchild.
I like to play piano, guitar, garden, have anoles, tree frogs, a gecko, and a toad, one dog, five cats and sometimes spiders. I collect rocks, crystals and gems. I like to make painted dragon eye rocks, and also I love muscle cars. I think I like just about everything that has to do with nature and animals.

I consider myself a wizard of sorts, because of the classes I've taken at the Grey School of Wizardry. I chose my own name, which is Stardragon. Stardragon is my wizardly name.
I think its a good thing, to have the name your parents gave you but also to have your own choice of a name that you chose for yourself.

I have also had two hives of honeybees, and I built the hives myself and got honey from them. Way too much honey!
I have had my own chickens and rabbits. Nothing is better then fresh eggs.
I learned to fish and hunt with my dad, so if the end of the world happens I know how to survive.

I write books and like to paint. I have painted watercolors of my dreams (mostly) and some other subject matter.
I do hand building with clay, and sell my crafts, sometimes I go to Native America pow-wows and sell them. I make mostly alien looking creatures, turtles, frogs, bowls, cups, air plant holders and some

jewelry and heat therapy bags. Cats love the heat bags, just warm them up and your cat is happy all day.

I also do painted stained glass and sell them at the shows and have done some for store windows.
I also do rug hooking. So a little bit of this and a little bit of that.

One of my greatest honors was being adopted by a member of the Pokanoket tribe as his adoptive daughter. It will be a day that I will never forget and treasure forever. I call him Father Hawk, and he will forever be in my heart. (he is on my right)

I have been running a book inmate service since 2002. Around that time I was contacted by a man, who had received a book from me in prison, he wrote and said that I should expand and sell books to inmates which I did. So I started from scratch at that time, and the business just grew and grew.

So I was busy doing this, then in 2003 I lost my daughter Lisa Jean at the young age of 27 in the Rhode Island Nightclub Station Fire, it was terrible. All I can say, is this work kept me going, it was the only thing I did that kept my mind off of my terrible loss. If it was for not hearing from all my "dragons" I don't think I could have done so well. Everyone was always writing, ordering books, telling me their problems, asking for advise keeping me busy, and sending me so much beautiful artwork.

So I kept on, and raised my daughter's beautiful little girl.
Even today I have some of my guys illustrating books for me. One favorite books is pictures of dragons done by many of my clients. If you ever want to check it out, its titled, "Dragon Art From Within The Dungeons."
All my books are available on Amazon.
My daughter, Lisa Jean, wrote a book about a year or less before the terrible tragedy. It was about two best friends and one dies. It was almost as if she wrote it for her daughter and us. We finally got that published for her, its titled, "Henry and Sara."

I have taken Fema classes and also am a ordained minister. (online if that counts) but I can marry someone and start my own church if I desired to do so legally.
 lol ! :-) lol !

I have been to Mt. Saint Helens in Washington and also been to the top of Mt. Washington in New Hampshire with my husband Greg. I have also been to Canada, and Germany.
I probable did other stuff, can't think of it now.

I was also able to do some professional modeling while in high school and after. One show I will remember was at Balfour, doing the run and having the camera's flashing. It was all pro on stage but in the back ground we were changing our outfits in the kitchen, that I will never forget.

If you want to know more about my childhood, I wrote a book titled: What It Was Like When I Was Little." All the family dirt is in that book!

Thanks for taking the time to read this collection and I hope you find some things that entertained you. So on with the stories and my view points on life, you might like them you might not. My granddaughter and me, laugh and call this my narcissist book, so you better like it! :-)

Life Lessons Only Two

Lesson one:
Wizards don't make new years resolutions, its not logical, everyone breaks them. In the long run, people just do what they want to do anyhow.

Lesson two.

Even though wizards don't make new years resolutions,
they are always working on being kind, generous and teaching others the things they know.
For example, learn about natural health, then when someone is ill you can pass on your knowledge of things that might help.
Learn about food, so you know what is good or not good for a person or wizard to consume.
Also if you are looking at someone, and you are thinking something nice about them, tell them. Like you might be thinking that they have nice earrings, the thought crossed your mind, so when that

happens you say, oh I like such and
such.
Never tell them the bad things you
are thinking about them, like oh
my! he has weird ears. got it?
These things work like a domino,
tip one over and it keeps on going.
Pass on wisdom,
until you hit a dud domino, and you
got to pick that one up, and start
all over!

Essay: The Name:
_____

I was named at birth Barbara Jean Ruggles. My middle name is not a
middle name, so I was always called Barbara Jean.
When I grew up, got married and moved then everyone that I met
from then on called me Barbara.
But whenever I went home, all the people that I knew and my
parents knew always called me Barbara Jean,
Then I got married so my last name changed, got divorced and
changed it back to my maiden name, got married again and now
have a new last name.
But for myself I always wanted to have my very own name that I
chose. I chose StarDragon as my own personal name quite a few
years ago. I thought it was important to choose one of my own liking
and that is what I did.

Most everyone calls me Barbara but a few friends do say StarDragon.

In my work, my business theme is with dragons and people account balances are called Dragon Gems. Some of my customers write to me as Dragon Keeper, Dragon Lady, Dragon Rider, Boston Barb, Barbara or Barbara Jean. Some even call me Auntie or Mom.

I work with inmates and buy books and provide services for them. After reading more about the different wizards and their names I see some will say Gandolf the Grey and so on, I read about the rainbow wizard. I never heard of that before, and it seems to fit for me. Even when I was little if you asked me what was my favorite color, I would say all the colors. I am into everything, and dab in all sorts of hobbies, and have worked in many different fields that I find anything and everything interesting. So I think maybe I should be StarDragon the Rainbow.

This is brand new for me, and I just feel its right for me.

I don't think I have outgrown any names that people choose to call me by. They are all a part of me. So its fine with me whatever names they choose to use.

A STORY

The Creature said to the man, "Oh, I think I will have you for dinner."

The man, who has the gift of speech replied, "But why? give me a good reason to kill and eat me."

The Creature said to the man, "Because, you are tasty."

The man said, "But that is not a good enough reason to kill me and take away my life."

The Creature replied to the man, "Well then, I have to feed my family."

The man said, "But that is still not a good enough reason either, meat is expensive and there are so many other things you can feed to your family."

The Creature said, " Well then, I have a recipe that calls for meat and I need meat to make it."

The man said, " That is still not good enough, you can make a different recipe, or make it without meat, or use something else instead of the meat. I am sure you are smart enough to figure it out."

The Creature replied back, " Well, I don't care, your tasty and I want meat!"

Well, logic did not work, and the man became the Creature's meal. Then the Creatures started to factory farm man. They built big buildings where they could breed man and make faster and faster large quantities of man to feed the masses. Soon man never saw the light of day, had no family or any sort of social life. One day the Creatures invented fertility drugs, so they could produce more. They also invented drugs to keep man from getting sick in overcrowded conditions. They also invented hormones to make man grow faster and bigger. And baby man was most tender and many were used for special dishes. Man was fed a diet of vegetables and also the waste parts of man. Nothing was wasted in the production of man, for profits meant everything to the Creatures.

This was all well for the Creatures as they got rich, had lots of food and were happy. Man was not.

Some Creatures rebelled against this unnatural way of keeping man and using him and his offspring for food. They rebelled against the way they were brought up, being taught to eat Man. Logically they did not understand why the other Creatures would want to eat something that is dead. This society of Creatures have always had a custom of burying the dead, so this did not make sense to them. So these rebellious Creatures started to live by only eating the vegetables and fruits of their planet. These Creatures became more healthy, and shiny and colorful. They did not know why, but enjoyed their new lives without eating Man.

Then one day far into the future, Man became toxic without the Creatures knowing it. And one day, all the Man eating Creatures died, all of them, all at once!

Then Man was free, they left the factory farms with the help of the Creatures that refused to eat Man. They build new lives and raised families. Practically overnight, this Planet became one of peace, Creatures and Man living together.

Being kind and loving each other, Creature and Man, Man and Creature.

Why Eat Meat?

It seems to me like if we eat an animal that even though we did not personally kill it, we contributed to its demise and mistreatment in the process of raising it for food.

The same thing with murder, we do not actually have to say, pull the trigger to get charged with murder, we only have to be involved in some way with the death of that person that was murdered.

So even though we are not actually killing the animal we are part of the process by buying it after it was killed.

The food system is run on supply and demand, if we stop buying a product there will be no need of it anymore. We need to realize that factory farms and big corporations only care about the money they are making. They do not care that these are living beings and not a disposable product that they can process for profit. it's just not right or moral.

Even though I know the killing of animals will probably never end or happen in my lifetime, I do not what to be a part of the process of cruelty to the animals that I think we all love.

And don't we love them? cows, pigs, chickens, lambs, turkeys? etc. We read about them as children, colored their pictures, and loved to go to petting zoos. Don't' we still love them? If we see a deer by the side of the road, or in the woods, we stop and say "look! how beautiful." or a little rabbit, we love seeing them, so why are we eating them? What changed?

So since not eating them anymore, I can't see why I ever wanted to, except besides the fact that I was brought up eating meat, and it tasted good. Even though I developed a taste for it, now I know better, I know what is really happening to these animals, and its a life they should not have to endure, just to be a tasty morsel on my plate. I think everyone has just as much right to be here and to enjoy their lives as anyone else and that includes all of us, even the animals.

There is so much to eat without meat.

So just do the best you can do, start out by eating less meat. Have meat free meals.

Just by doing that it can make a big difference. :-)

PUTTING SMOKEY TO SLEEP

We had to put my daughters cat Smokey to sleep. It was very sad losing such a wonderful little animal. He was a great cat, grey in color with big beautiful green eyes and so affectionate.

The staff at the vets were very compassionate and kind, everyone felt bad.

He was gently put to sleep with lots of love and petting.
Later that made me reflect, thinking of how much we love our pets and all animals in general. We never would want to see them suffer or have any pain or be unhappy.

Then I pictured what was going on in the real world, with all the farm animals, and is still going on, right now while you are reading this. Thousands of animals are being slaughtered, and not in a kind gentle way.

No kinds words or petting for them. Raised in horrible factory farm conditions, trucked for miles, some even freeze on the way to the slaughterhouses, stuck to the sides of the trucks, and the ones that can walk are lined up for the slaughter. How sad, waiting in line to be killed.

Why is humanity so cruel to the ones we eat and so kind to the ones we call pets?

To me it is a heartbreaking situation. I think because we cannot see what is happening, we think it does not happen and we just don't think or care enough to do something about it. Out of sight, out of mind. So is that where humans stand right now? Not caring enough, just pushing it aside, and going on their happy ways. Cooking meat, thinking it is so great and not knowing what it really is?

To me its eating cruelty, sadness, fear, and loss of spirituality, and just not caring enough about the lives of innocent animals. There is so much to eat without meat.

Meat is not meat, meat is a living being, a cow, a pig, a turkey a rabbit, a horse, a lamb. It's not a product made out of plastic, its a living feeling creature. Next time you walk by the meat counter, think of where it came from, and the suffering it caused some little animal. Think about the life of that animal and what it went through to end up in a meat counter.

Someday I pray, that what is happening will reach everyone's heart and the slaughter will end for these wonderful animals.

The most stupid question I have been asked about not eating animals was, "If we don't eat them what will we do with them all?"

THINGS I GET

ASK OR THINK ABOUT IT AND IT WILL COME TO YOU (gifts from the universe)

My daughter, Lisa Jean taught me about asking the universe for things you need, and that they will just show up.
I remember her needing a pair of skates and one day she came home with a nice pair, they were on the side of the road she told me.
So I took her advise and when I was looking for something I needed, I would just put it out to the universe and forget about it. Sure enough things would somehow show up.

Some examples that have happened:

Dining Room.
I needed a buffet, I thought about it an then went to Savers, and there it was, just what I wanted, in fine condition for only 15.00

Then I was thinking I would like a extra chair for my white table set. As I was driving up the street, there it was on the side of the road, like new, a perfect match, for free. I drove right by it, as I hate to stop and pick up stuff on the side of the road, but as I drove past it, I was thinking, oh, the universe got my chair, I can't just drive by it, so I turned around and went back and got it. I am so happy I did, it was just right.

On another day I was thinking it would be nice to have a china closet or something for my dishes that would be covered so they did not get dusty. I was even thinking of where to put it if I got one. I was thinking how to arrange things in my room if I got one and the thought popped into my mind: Salvation Army. So I went there in Pawtucket and there it was for less then twenty bucks.

I was thinking that I would like my sister to come up to visit from Florida. It would be so nice if she could see my new dining room. I knew she would love it, but I know that would not happen as she was up here in the spring and no way would she fly back from Florida again this time of year, as her cooking business gets busy right now until next spring. Then out of nowhere she calls me, her tooth broke, her dentist down in Florida said 3000 to fix it, so that was too much. She called my daughter, Destiny who worked at a dental office to see if they can fix it. They gave her a family discount and my sister flew up here the next week and got her tooth fixed. What an unexpected surprise.

Back a few years ago, I thought I would like a door for my office to keep the cats out. I asked my son if I bought a door would he put it up, and of course he said yes.
Greg and I took a walk around the neighborhood and laying right on someone's front lawn was a door. It looked like just what I pictured.

I asked the people if I could have it and they say yes. Greg and I took it home and it fit perfectly.

Then my son said to me, "are you sure you want that door? I can get a new one for you," I told him, "are you crazy I am not going to argue with the universe."

One day I thought it would be nice to have a sewing machine table. So I was telling my son about it, and then he started looking on Amazon for one for me.

In the meantime on my way to the post office there was a sewing machine table on the side of the road. It needed to be painted and needed new knobs and a cover the the drawer area, but other then that it was fine. I knocked on the ladies door and asked her about it, and she said I could take it.

So I took it home and snuck it into my room, I did not want my son to see it until I fixed it up. It did not take long, I painted it white, it looked brand new. When Joe saw it, he could not believe that I just got it off the side of the road. I told him, the universe always gets you what you want.

I wanted so much to be a part of the Native American family, I even got my blood DNA done to see if I had any Native American heritage. It came back that I was not. Then one weekend when we were at a Native American Pow-wow with my daughter selling crafts, I met a few tribe members and one man was so nice and talkative so I told him and his brother how I felt. He right then told me their history and asked me some questions and adoptive me as his daughter. It was the most thrilling moment in my life. I could hardly contain my tears of joy.

Since then every year I see him at the pow-wow, and he comes looking for us at our craft tent. He is in his eighties, and dresses in the traditional clothes, and he wears mostly purple. I love watching him dance in the circle with his brother and grandson.

So come to find out, my grandfather's line comes directly from the Battle Of Hastings and the Norman Conquest in 1066, and the name Ruggles comes from the name of the village that people that helped came from. It was fought between the Norman-French army of William, the Duke of Normandy, and the English army under the Anglo-Saxon King Harold Godwinson. This battle was the beginning of the Norman conquest of England. So my line does comes from warriors after all, the Vikings! There is a most beautiful book about it, titled, "The Bayeux Tapestry. It contains the illustrations of the battle embroidered on cloth 230 feet long and 20 inches tall. It details the events leading up to the battle and ending with the Battle of Hastings.

Today after a big rain storm last night it seemed that turtles were out crossing the roads. My daughter called me told mean that she and two friends all saved a turtle crossing the road.

Well I have a small pond in my yard and I would have liked to find a turtle too. But was not about to go out looking for one.

Later in the day, my son was sitting out in the yard and he said to look over near the fence (our yard is fenced in) there was a nice sized sun turtle. How in the world did he get there? He must have come from the river across a busy street and dug under my fence to get into my yard.

Thank you universe

SAGE

My intention is to use the herb sage to cleanse my living space with positive energy.

I had bought a bundle of sage from our local pow-wow this past summer.

I have a large quahog shell and I am going to use this to carry the sage in as it burns.

I have lit the sage on fire with a match and have let it burn for a few minutes before blowing out the flames. I have a few embers that are smoking giving off a great fragrance.

I like to start at one end of my home and smudge it room by room till I get to the other end. As I am doing this I carry the shell with the burning sage in one hand and with the other hand I push the smoke out towards the walls and ceiling. As I do this I am saying positive things like, please clear this area of any negative energy, allowing good thoughts and love to be presence. I also say that any good spirits of my family and pets are are allowed in this space. I repeat this in all my rooms. I also do my sunroom where people enter my home. I ask that the people leave behind any negative energy and to enter my home with love.

Once I am done I leave the sage to burn in the shell till it burns out.

It is interesting to note, that after doing this when my husband arrives home from work he will say, "Did you clean the house today? It smells so clean."

Sage is used to make medicine such as dietary supplements for digestion problems, a sore mouth and throat, and memory loss and depression. The sage leaves and extracts are available as liquids, throat sprays, lozenges and capsules.

The two most common kinds of sage are Salvia Officials and Spanish Sage or Salvia Lavandulaefolia.

It is interesting to note that sage has some great nutrients. It contains magnesium, phosphorus, potassium, folate, beta-carotene, vitamin A and vitamin K.
And you can use sage in soups, stuffing and you can mix it with butter to make sage butter.

Even though sage is awesome it also contains Thujone which can affect your nervous system. If you use too much or use the oil of sage you may get bad side effects such as vomiting, vertigo, rapid heartbeat, tremors, seizures and even kidney damage.

The smoke has rapid effect to the brain and efficient absorption to the body.
This is what causes it to have a good mood effect on our brains.
I find it interesting that sage smoke can clear up to 94 percent of airborne bacteria and clean the air. This is good to remember in flu and cold seasons.

I think it would be interesting if they did a study on the effects of burning sage in places that have high levels of negativity or crime.

It could be tested in a prison, or hospital, or a school system to see how people would respond. Sage might be the answer to a million social problems. I do notice at the pow-wows when sage is burning I always feel so happy to smell it burning and it is always a happy peaceful place to be.

Also I use sage to smudge my whole yard perimeter anytime we are getting a hurricane. I also do it for my sisters house in Florida, even though she is a thousand miles from me, I will go outside in my yard, and make a vision of her home in yard in my mind, and sage it. If you saw me walking around my yard doing this, you would probably think I was crazy. I am walking around her house, inside and out, just like it was there.
So far in all our hurricanes nothing has been damaged, the most I get is a few small sticks or branches from the neighbors yard. My trees were all fine every time.
My sister thinks I am crazy too, but after a hurricane she calls me and says, the trailer park has branches and trees down everywhere, but my yard is fine, only a few twigs. :-)

The People I Trust To Tell Me The Truth

 The first people in my life I trusted to tell me the truth were my parents. If they did something to not gain that trust I think I would have ruined my trust of all people for the rest of my life. I would always be double checking what someone told me. Parents by being truthful and trusting give children the ability to also be trusting and truthful.

But since I never found any untruths that my parents told me, It has made me a trustworthy person. And I usually believe what everyone tells me until I find out differently or I do some research and find out differently.

If I found out differently, it would be either because they were wrongly told or being deceitful, and that I would find out by talking to them.

The next people in my life I trusted to tell me the truth were close friends.

When you share your life with someone and keep secrets as children do, you come to trust your friends.

Then, family like brothers and sisters, grandparents, your husband or wife, you expect them to teach you the truth in life. Especially if they are older then you, that makes them smarter in your eyes right away. And being brought up to respect your elders, made you think they knew everything, and of course, would never lie!

Teachers, we always believed our school teachers as children. But as I got older I think I questioned what they said more. If it conflicted with what my parents taught me, I would think they were wrong. I remember a teacher teaching us about evolution and how we came from apes, well that was not what I was taught and me and my best friend would laugh about it, thinking the teacher was so crazy.

I was brought up to respect the law, so I trusted the police and anyone in authority to tell me the truth.

Until someone gave me reason not to trust the knowledge they extended my way, I would take it at face value.

But I would always do my own research and find out more information on a subject if I needed it.

Today I like to believe what people say, and do, but always knowing they might have information that might not always be exact, I do my own research still, so it's always worth your time to do your own research.

Also using my own instinct on whether it sounds logical or not, or if any red flags pop up in the conservation. Or any body language that makes me feel that the person does not know what he or she is talking about, or they are giving out bad vibrations.

Some of the ways to test if something is true, is by going to the library and getting books on the subject. Going on the internet. Asking more than one person to see if they come up with the same answers, and thinking for yourself, and asking does this seem right? If its a morale question, you know if its right or wrong, without someone telling you. So you have to depend on yourself for answers too.

In general I will ask questions for example on how to build something to get the other persons ideas, but then I go ahead and follow some of their suggestions or use my own. But in the end I always make up my own mind.

Knowledge that I possess that I got from someone else.

My dad taught me to pick wild mushrooms, and to pick the ones that were safe to eat. I trusted him completely and ate everyone he picked. What surprises me today is that I can take someone to the woods and pick mushrooms and they will happily eat them without question. Now would I do that with someone I know today? no, I would not.

 Doctors, we are brought up to trust them, but I study many different forms of healing and nutrition and doctors just don't know it all. Drug companies pressure them to prescribe their products. Example: when I was diagnosed with Osteoporosis, my doctor prescribed this bone medication. So I went online and found out what it did and did not do. It had many side effects such a actually making your bones weaker, so I choose not to take it. I found another product that makes your bones stronger with no side effects. After four years I did my bone test again, and my bones have improved.

At my next doctors appointment he said to me, oh that bone medication, you cannot take it anymore as it is causing bones to break. I never took it anyhow, but that just proves that is important to do your own research.

I think its important to listen to people and what they share with you, to take in their knowledge and blend it with your own. Not everything is black and white.

To listen to what they say, and then after, question it if you are not sure of what they are saying. I have said to people many times, "are you sure about that?"

So you do not want to be distrusting of what people tell you, but do your own research and make up your own mind. And I think its important to be flexible, so once you make up your mind, and you learn new truths you can change what you believe.

WEIRD THINGS/OTHER DIMENSIONS

Things in other dimensions
that I have seen or noticed over the years.
I bought this house, in 1980 which was built in the 1960's and have been here ever since. I have heard rumors that a boy who lived here drowned in the Ten Mile River.

I am calling this "other dimensions" as I cannot explain them as occurring, in this dimension they make no sense, so the "other" seems to be more explainable.

I am relating these in the times I remember them.

The Frog Pond. (about 10 years ago)
we have a man made frog pond that I built myself, and my sister and Greg helped build the second pond. It has two sections. each about 8 ft. by 9 ft. And they were just relined with brand new liners.
The pond was recently filled.
The next morning I went out, and the front half was practically empty.
Where did all the water go? I checked for leaks, none, no water on the ground around the edges.
I refill the pond to the top, and it never happened again until about ten years later, 2023, when I got up in the morning one side was almost empty, I filled it and it has been fine since.

The Circle (about 11 years ago)

In our driveway, it is covered with small rocks, which we had put there for our driveway for drainage.

Our driveway is on a hill.

One day I went out, and there was a circle about 12 x 12 inches in diameter.

It looked like the inside of the circle was vacuumed, as there was not a bit of sand or stone left. It was hard like cement on the bottom. The edges were a perfect looking circle.

How it got there I have no idea. I have a picture of this that I saved and some of the dirt from the outside edges.

Lightning (nothing strange about it)
but I have seen it hit the top of my driveway two times. The only reason I saw it was I was standing on my sunporch at the time.

Drops of Water (throughout the years)

The first time drops of water fell on me, I was sitting on one of the kids beds. Then a drop of water fell on my arm. I do not know where it came from. The ceiling was not wet or had any condensation on it.

The second time, years later, I was in my bedroom talking to Greg when a few drops fell on my arm. Same thing, no water on the ceiling or condensation.

Water also fell on a friend that was over visiting my granddaughter. They were in the room in the cellar. They came running upstairs as quite a few drops of water fell on his neck. We thought maybe water leaked from upstairs, but nothing was on the floor above them, and when we looked at the floor boards where it happened down cellar it was not wet, none of the pipes ha water on them, no drops no condensation. Nothing was damp or wet.

A year ago. in the same room, which is now a workroom, water fell on my son, he was confused as he could not figure our where it came from.

I once was folding clothes in the cellar, in the laundry room. The other refinished room in the cellar had a piano, every so often I would hear a note played

Folding clothes in the cellar, in the laundry room, which is right down the stairs from the kitchen, and the kitchen door.
I heard one of the kids come in, and our dog walk across the floor. I called out, hi, and went right upstairs. No one was there.

Google earth shows our address on the wrong side of the street.

In 2014 we lost our cat, Skye. This summer I was in my bedroom, Baby our cat was sitting on the VHS. I talked to her, and went into the kitchen to get something off the counter. As I walked by the sliding glass doors, on the deck was Baby sitting there with her back towards me. I thought to myself. Wow Baby, you sure are fast, how did you get out there so fast. I went back into the bedroom, and Baby was still on the VHS. Since Baby and Skye looked a lot alike, I

think I saw Skye sitting on the deck. I went right back to look out on the deck and the cat was gone.
(baby is a slow moving cat)

This past week, I seem to be seeing more things.
I was at my desk, and it faces the window to the street. I have some bamboo outside the window but I can see the street through it.
I saw a jogger run by, and then start back, so being noisy I stood up to get a better look, to see who it was, and they went half way back, and than was the jogger was gone.
I don't know where he went.

This past week, I was in the living room, walking out to the office. the rooms are separated by a wall. So between the two rooms, I can see out both windows. At this point of looking out both windows I saw out the office window a white delivery truck coming up my street, so I wanted to see if they would stop and deliver a package at my house. So I stood between the two rooms and waited to see if the truck would stop. Well it never went by. So between the window in my office and the wall, it just disappeared. So I went and looked out the window. No truck.

Today I was sitting at my kitchen table eating oatmeal, looking into the living room.
I can see Heaven our white cat in there, and I see Simba, our cat walk by the exercise machine towards the front door, I went to get him and put him out as he has a habit of marking. So I get up to go get him and as I walk by my office, I see our kitten on the rug. I go

to get Simba and he is not by the front door, so I figure he ran behind the couch, he is not there, so he must be somewhere, yes, I go look everywhere and he is sound asleep on the bed in the bedroom with Rusty and Baby.

A long time ago, Greg was out at a gig, and I stayed home. I was just woken up late at night by Zoe Jean and went in and laid down with her to get her back to sleep. Then I heard Greg came in the door from the gig and I did not say anything as I did not want to wake up Zoe Jean, but he kept saying, "What? What?"
so I got up and went into the kitchen, and told him to be quite, Zoe Jean just went back to sleep and why was he saying What? What? he told me, he heard someone calling his name.

Sitting in my office, looking out the window, someone walking up the street, with a sweatshirt hoodie coat, walked halfway past my window, and was gone, I got up went outside and looked up and down the street. no one was there, so another person going by that does not complete the walk by.

It's been some time since I have written anything but this occurrence needs to be documented. I have a tank with two tree frogs in my bedroom.
It has a door on the front that locks and a top that has a screen which is clipped in and does not move and also taped. There is no way for a frog to get out.

On some occasions when feeding or cleaning the cage, the door will be open and one of the free frogs has leaped straight out onto my shirt or arm.

This week I bought a new spray bottle so when I mist them I do it right through the screen right on the top of the cage that way I do not have to open their door.

Lasts night before I went to bed I was admiring the bright green frog stretched out on a branch. Then I got ready for bed and just before I shut off their light I sprayed the tank through the screen. At that time I only saw one frog, but you don't always see them as they tend to hide.

In the morning when I opened the shade next to the table with the frog tank I noticed on the side of the table something that resembled rat poop. I thought that is so weird there would not be a rat in the house, at least I hoped it was not so.

So I took a shower, got dressed and was looking at the tank and I noticed something on the container that is on the floor next to the tank. Right on the cover was the bright green tree frog. I picked him up and put him back into the tank. The door was still locked and I checked that top and it was secure. I cannot figure out how he got out of the tank. At least now I know it was not rat poop but only a frog turd.

BUILDING A BIRD FEEDER

I love to feed the birds and have done that my whole life. I learned about the birds from my mother.

Of course when you feed birds you always run into problems with squirrels overtaking the bird feeder.

So years ago my sister told me how to build a squirrel proof bird feeder, which I built and I still have it today. I even wrote a book on how to do that. "How To Build A Squirrel Proof Bird Feeder."
But I want to put up more bird feeders without having to build the bigger one.
I wanted to put up the little feeders and the round ball type ones that just hold the sunflower seeds.

So I have been thinking of a way to do another feeder by hanging a rope from a tree branch high enough so that the squirrels could not jump onto it either from the top or the ground. But the problem was refilling the feeder once it was hung up.

This took some thought and I figured I could tie something heavy to one end of a rope and throw it up over a branch.
Once I got it over I could put on a hook and hang my bird feeder from one end and pull the rope up until the bird feeder was high enough off the ground.
The other end of the rope I tied to a hook I put on a the tree it was hanging from.
Now when I have to fill the bird feeder I just unhitch the rope and lower the feeder, refill it and pull it back up.

This is working out fine, the birds are happy, and the squirrels still eat what the birds spill or drop.

Turmeric Tonic

Recipe was written by Alison Roman from
bonappetit.com.

You need:
12 inch piece of peeled turmeric
12 inch piece of peeled ginger
1/2 lemon
3 tablespoons agave syrup (nectar)
Sparkling water
Cayenne pepper

(dash of black pepper) (not in original recipe, my suggestion)

I learned that by adding cayenne pepper to food it boosts your metabolism and helps with circulation. But I noticed that the recipe does not contain black pepper as the tea recipe does.
I found that by adding black pepper to a tea or tonic it helps enhances the bioavailability of many drugs including turmeric. Studies have shown that by adding just a little black pepper with turmeric it can boost the levels of curcumin by up to 2,000%. If you are making the tonic I suggest adding a dash of black pepper.

Grate the turmeric, ginger and lemon (with peel) through a juicer.
Stir in agave syrup.
Or you can chop the turmeric and ginger and puree it in a blender with the agave syrup and add 2 tablespoons of fresh lemon juice and 1/3 cup of water then strain.
Serve the juice over ice topped off with sparkling water and sprinkle with cayenne pepper.

Turmeric has antioxidant and anti-inflammatory properties and can help with digestion. In western medicine they have been studying it to see how it can help with gut inflammation and digestion.
It has been scientifically proven to help prevent heart disease, Alzheimers and cancer. It may also help with depression and arthritis and to prevent kidney stones.

By adding ginger to the tonic it adds in the benefits to settle and reduce nausea and helps with digestion. Ginger has also been shown to slow down the progression of multiple types of cancers especially the ones in the gastrointestinal system.
The combination of the two helps manage diabetes as there is a blood sugar regulating abilities in these two roots.

Ginger and turmeric have also been found to boost brain cognition and to also help fight again some neurological diseases.

Ginger and turmeric also contain iron, calcium, magnesium and copper.

You can also make tea:
1 cup of hot water
1 teaspoon of ginger
1 teaspoon of turmeric
1 teaspoon of honey or lemon
1 teaspoon of black pepper

There are no guidelines as to when to add spices to a child's diet and you should ask your pediatrician, but these types of aromatic spices have been used in other cultures in children's diets from a early age on. There was one study that in children between the ages of 11-18 with inflammatory bowel disease were given Curcumin, (one of the active components of
turmeric) and the study found it to be well tolerated by the children.

References:
medicalnewstoday.com
Standardmedia.com
bonappetit.com
wiki.com

Foxglove

I have it growing in my garden and it was one of my mother's favorite flowers.
The butterfly and hummingbirds love it.

Foxglove grows throughout the United States, wild and cultivated. It also grows in Europe, Asia and Africa.
The flowers are bell-shaped and usually a bright purple but I have seen it in all colors such as a creamy yellow, pink and rose. They bloom in the spring on tall spikes.

The name foxglove is named after a man in 1542 by the name of Leonhard Fuchs, and the name Fuchs in German is the word for "fox".

It was once in a folk myth that the foxes wore the flowers on their paws so they would be quiet as they hunted.

The scientific name for Foxglove is Digitalis Purpurea which is the common foxglove plant.
There are about twenty species of it in the form of perennials, shrubs and biennials.
The name digitalis is interesting because it means finger-like and that is because the flower fits easily over a human fingertip. :-)
That was interesting.

There word digitalis is also used for drugs that contain cardiac glycosides.
So it is used to treat heart problems.

But even though it is good in medical use it can also be toxic to humans and animals.

If you have a overdose of digitalis it can cause nausea, vomiting and diarrhea and also jaundice, drooling, tremors seizures and even death.

Herbalists have stopped using it because of the difficulty of knowing how much to use to be safe. Because it can also cause deadly results is has also been called dead man's bells and witch's gloves. The entire plant is toxic including the roots and seeds. Sometimes people confuse this plant with comfrey which is used to make tea, with really bad results. Children have died from drinking the water from a vase that contains foxglove and drying does not reduce its effects. This plant is toxic to all animals.

References:
www.poison.org
Wiki

Demons

I personally do not think that being a Wizard that it would be a good practice to trap a djinn into any form of service, even if it was for good only.

If you did trap a djinn into service, even if it wanted to do your bidding, it is ruled by Iblis the Prince of Darkness, so if you took one of the djinn's he rules over, you might be messing around with not such a good demon.
I also think this would be a form of slavery to use another entity to force it to do your bidding.

Plus we don't really know that if trapping a djinn makes them untrustworthy and violent. They are considered evil by nature but I don't think we would know for sure unless we worked with one.
I don't think it would be a good thing to do just to answer this question.

I always thought from what I learned, that demons had free will so they could obey God or they could choose their own path. Because they questioned God, saying they should be worshipped just as God himself is worshipped, they caused the war in heaven and that is why they were thrown out of heaven and lots of angels went with them.

To begin with these demons were angels and because they did not obey God they were now considered demons. Just because that happened I don't think that all demons might be evil in nature as they did not start out that way.

They could be indifferent to us or might like to cause problems for mankind.
It seems people have a way of causing many of their own problems without any outside help.
And it might be easy to make an excuse for things not going the right way by saying the devil made me do it.

In any case, it would not be wise for a Wizard to get the help from outside sources such as a djinn or any sort of demon.

Becoming An Apprentice

I have learned many important lessons in a interesting class I took, Becoming An Apprentice Wizard.

I will be able to share the difference between a wizard and a sorcerer, as some people think wizards are evil so that I can just point out the difference between us, so if they want to think of anyone as evil it would be a person who considers him or herself a sorcerer. Wizards are there to be of service but sorcerers want to be served.

I also realized that it is important to be a part of the community and to bring positive vibes to the lives of people around us. This is something I am working on more to be out there and
to share my knowledge and to listen well. I have tried to donate more goods to places nearby, bring sick people food and to be there out in the open to offer a helping hand. I run a book service and I have listed the Grey School Grimoires so people can order them.

I learned about riding the waves and to be able to look ahead, and this I found was a good teaching tool for my children is that you do not have to live in the exact moment, and react, like flipping out if you don't get you own way, you can look ahead to see what the results of your actions will bring. Like no dessert tonight! I think that be being calm and thinking what the waves will bring, is so much better then just reacting, stop and listen and by your example you are teaching others. It does not always have to be with your voice.

I liked the story of being in the dark cave and that what we learn we need to share, and we are not losing any knowledge by doing so, we are growing when we keep learning and teaching others what we know. That was a great lesson and in turn we need to share our knowledge.

I always talk to my children about everything because if we don't tell them what we know they will not know of it. Even when my kids did not seem interested like when I was gardening I would point out the different plants and show them the bugs. I always felt it was important do do this, so many things my mom told me I forgot, until I was in the middle of say, cooking a stew and all of a sudden I could hear my mom's voice saying, make sure when you do this you brown the onions well. It so funny how what others tell us will come to us when we need to know something. It is so important we share what we know.

I loved the lesson on creating my personal alter, it is a place of peace and a place where I can set my intentions. This helps me to keep my course of what I want to do and the kind of person and or wizard I want to be.

Learning about a magical name was interesting to write about, leaning that we have many names in our lives and picking out my own that I felt comfortable with. Telling my family about it and some of them are picking out there own personal names.

There is so much to share in these classes that are important to me and I am sure I will share the things I have learned more and more as time goes by.

This journey of learning is certainly interesting and I just love these classes.

I also was encourage to submit a work of my writing to Grey Matters and they published it this week, it is titled " The Great Tree Meditation". Thank you for encouraging me to do that.

Ghosts

I have a few local ghost stories I can share with you. They were told to me by a friend of the family, a person who I have know for years. Her name is June Young and she grew up in the area of the stories.

I did not grow up in this area and it was exciting to hear the stories and of course we have visited the sites many times throughout the years, hoping to catch a glance of the ghosts but no luck so far.

One story is about the Shad Factory Pond located in Seekonk MA. She told me that sometimes people would see a man dressed in a cloak along the shores of this pond. Also glowing orbs and lights shining in the woods.
A long time ago there was a mill at the waterfall at the end of the pond. The mill burned down two times. It was a cotton mill.
They say the mill is haunted. My friend never said that anyone died there but I think probably someone did if they are seeing a cloaked figure.
If there is a ghost there I think it would be a ghost that died in the fire, as in a accident. He might still be there at the that site. It could also be a psychic impression of the violent death in the fire.

Another story she told me about was the haunted Hornbine School, which is located in Rehoboth Ma.

The school was used until 1937. Then it was turned into a historic site. People who visit it have seen a ghost of a school teacher wearing a dress from the looks of it like back in the 1800's style. They also say they have seen young children. It looks like they are just repeating their actions over and over again.

I think that is these ghosts are repeating whatever they are doing over and over again makes it sounds like a psychic impression.

My friend also told me about the ghost on route 44 in Rehoboth MA. Which she said she has seen herself. Some people when driving on a certain section of south 44 will see a red headed man hitchhiking. He also wears a red flannel shirt. No one knows who he was but everyone thinks maybe he was hit by a car and killed. People that have stopped to give him a ride said he disappears or if he gets in the car he soon disappears. Some people say when driving there if they are listening to the radio they hear a man screaming and laughing.
There are lots of stories about this ghost.
I think this would be called a "haunt".

Another place in Rehoboth is Anawan Rock, which is now a historical site where the Native American War Chief Anawan chief of the Pocasset People, was captured by the British, which ended the King Phillips War in 1676.

In the 1920's and 1930's it was a popular place for picnics and hiking in the woods.

People at that time started to say they saw apparitions of Native American men and women, hearing voices and screams and chanting. Some people saw orbs and ghost fires late at night.
I am not sure what kinds of ghosts these would be. We have gone there many times, its a beautiful site with huge boulders taller then a house.

Palmer River Cemetery is located in Rehoboth MA. People say they see a little boy dressed in 1800 style clothes running around in the cemetery. The also have heard voices, footsteps and a young child crying. It is located in a remote wooded area.
I think this would be considered real ghosts. My daughter and I spent an afternoon in the cemetery and we painted pictures.

I also have a ghost story of my own, I had a bedroom down cellar and a closet with door that has beads as curtains. One night I was reading my book in bed and heard noises in the closet, so I thought it was the cat. I went upstairs and my husband was watching tv and the cat was sleeping on the couch. I asked him how long the cat was there and he said all night. I thought that was strange and went back to bed, but as I was reading my book I kept one eye on the closet.

Soon enough I heard noises again and then the strangest thing happened. The beads were lifted up, like someone grabbed a handful and lifted them up and then just dropped them. That is when I ran upstairs and told my husband what had happened. He said it must be the wind. I was like, what, there is no wind in the cellar.
I went back to bed. I am not afraid of ghosts.

I have also had water drop on my arm in the bedroom, and years later again in another room.

A few years ago my son had water fall on him in the cellar and it also happened to one of my granddaughter's friends. We have no leaks at all anywhere.

I heard the story somewhere that before we bought our home, some child drowned in the Ten Mile River near our home. I always think that maybe it is his spirit.

To me these seem like real ghosts.

I have also heard people come into my house with a dog, and have even yelled out, hey, Derek I am downstairs, only to go upstairs and find no kid or dog.

So my friend told me most of these stories and I only looked them up to find out the exact locations and time periods.

Self-Cleansing and Clearing Your Personal Space

I like to use sage to clean my area as I do this I like to say, "with this smoke make this place safe and for negative energies to leave. Protect those living here and make this a happy place."

I will say this as I sage each area in my home or where I have my altar.

When I want to clean my body and space I like to take a hot shower and use pine scented soaps. The smell of the soap, evergreen reminds

me of Christmas trees and just breathing in the scent makes me feel so good, its amazing. As I breathe in that scent all stress just seems to leave me immediately and makes me smile. Washing my skin with a loofah sponge feels so refreshing my skin glows.
After the refreshing shower I like to put on something comfortable, even pajamas, making me feel relaxed.

Then after I am dressed I like to light my candles at my altar and light a sage bundle and proceed to clean the altar area saying the words I wrote,
"with this smoke make this place a safe and for all negative energies to leave. Protect those living here and make this a happy place"
Then I like to brush the smoke on myself with my hand sweeping it towards myself and up and down my body. I like breathing in the smell of the sage. It is a smell that I enjoy. It has a relaxing and calming effect to me. It also reminds me of going to the pow-wow's we have in our area. It's such a wonderful feeling there being outside and smelling that drifting through the air.
After I do this I am ready to make any intentions I have planned for that day.

The definitions of Widdershins and Deosil are: In Scottish folklore, sunwise, deosil or sunward (clockwise) was considered the "prosperous course", turning from east to west in the direction of the sun. The opposite course, counterclockwise, was known as widdershins (Lowland Scots), or tuathal (Scottish Gaelic).
Which I found at en.wikipedia.or/sunwise

So when doing my cleaning with my sage I always go with Deosil, turning clockwise. I just do it this way out of habit.

When I go into my room to clean it I start at the left of the door and proceed around the room clockwise.

It is interesting to note, that when I do a sage ritual in my house and I don't tell anyone, when my husband comes home he will say, did you clean the house today ? Which I did not actually clean, I had only used the sage.

I feel that it is important to do the self cleaning to make yourself feel relaxed and stress free. I do this to my house at lease once per month and I do this before I do any intentions at my altar. So cleansing my home is part of my mundane life and my intentions are part of my magical practices.

I even do the sage ritual for my sister at my home for her home in Florida every time they get a hurricane. I go out into my yard and I use my chicken pen as a guide to her house. I can picture her house inside and out as I walk around with and I sage her whole property, each room inside and the outside buildings. I always say, as I push the smoke out towards the room I am picturing, going clockwise, or Deosil, around her house and property, protect this house from harm and keep the winds away, I also push the smoke out toward the palm trees behind her house up towards them and say, "keep these trees strong and protect them from breaking and falling over. Keep the winds away from here."

This takes quite a bit of energy to do, but I do it at least three times per day as the storm approaches her. So far, when she comes back to her home she has had no damage or trees down, even though her neighbors do.

Nettle

I have heard it makes a Nettle makes a healthy tea for women and I would like to know more about it. So I did some research and here is what I found.

From the Woden's Nine Herbs Charm it says that Nettle protects against poison and expels malignant things. It is the herb that fought against the serpent, it avails against contagion.
It sounds like a very powerful herb.

Nettle is a shrub that comes from northern Europe and Asia.
The plant is pretty, with heart shaped leaves and yellow or pink flowers.
Nettle is also called stinging nettle, it's latin name is Urtica Dioica. This word means "to burn" because its leaves can cause a burning sensation upon contact and the stem is covered in tiny stiff hairs that releases the stinging chemical when touched. The chemical that causes the burning sensation is formic acid, and the leaves also contain histamine and other chemicals. The antidote to the sting is from a plant called Dock leaf, and the sap contains a antihistamine which helps when applied to the skin of a person that has been affected by the nettles burn.

Nettle has health benefits too. It contains many nutrients. If you make nettle tea it contains vitamin A, various B vitamins such as B-1,, B-2. B-3 and B-5. Vitamin C, amino acids, calcium, fatty acids, folic acid, iron, magnesium, manganese, phosphorus and potassium.

Drinking the tea may reduce inflammation, treat enlarged prostate symptoms, hay fever, lower blood pressure and help in blood sugar control. Nettle teas is also perfect for sodium induced water retention and it flushes the kidneys and bladder to prevent and soothe urinary tract infections.

The roots also contain nutrients such as vitamins A, C and K and many B vitamins, minerals, calcium, iron, magnesium, phosphorus, potassium and sodium. It also contains fats such as linoleic acid, linoleric acid, palmitic acid, stearic acid and oleic.

Nettle has been used for hundreds of years to treat painful muscle and joints, eczema, arthritis, gout and anemia. Today people use it for urinary problems in the early stages of enlarged prostrate issues.

In Greek times they used it mainly as a diuretic and laxative. Today they even use it in hair and skin products.

To make nettle tea take your nettle leaves and heat to a near boil. Do not boil tea. Use about two cups of water to a cup of leaves. You can make it stronger by stepping it longer, or weaker by adding more water. Once the water is near boiling turn off the heat. I like to put my leaves in a cup and then add boiling water. This prevents me boiling it by mistake.

You can also make a nettle infusion. To do this you need 1/3 cup of dried organic nettle, 1 liter of water. Boil the water and pour over the dried nettle leaves. Allow to sit overnight or at least 4 hours.

I am amazed at the many health benefits of nettle. It is one of the wonders of the herb world and I can fully understand why it was included in Woden's Nine Herbs Charm.
The other herbs included in the charm are: mugwort, watercress, betonyi, chamomile, crabapple, chervil and fennel chamomile. There are others that are also used depending on the area. There are Norse and Celtic which have a few different herbs used
Such as Plantain, lambs cress, betony, and chervil.

Drones

Its like the movie terminator.
I knew they had drones to take pictures of places and to fly over enemy territory to see what was going on, but had no idea that they could use them to shoot people or drop bombs.
I guess they figure they can save soldiers lives by sending the drones into battle instead of the soldiers getting killed.

But to see them used to target people at home and then bombing them is so wrong, killing innocent family members.

Thinking about it all it shows what a primitive people we are. So much violence. No one learned anything from history. We take it as normal but if you look at it, its so true.
After all these thousands of years why are people still fighting and killing each other? We think we are advanced, but in reality we are not at all.

I would not be surprised if an advanced race will wipe us all out before we have a chance to go to another planet and take it over and start a war just to get their resources. I guess if you listen to War Pigs by Black Sabbath it hits it right on the mark.
I use to listen to that when I was a teenager and hated the government so much, it was so true and it is even today.

All the leaders in all the countries spend trillions to make weapons just to kill each other. That money could be used for so many other things to help the human race, but no, war is never going to end unless they stop killing each other. So what is all this fighting about? Its about greed, religion, racism, and the leaders in control wanting to be in power. Thinking they are the right ones to say what others can do or not do.
Or any stupid reason a bully might have to terrorize or hurt someone else. The government steps in to say protect the weak that are being taken over by a bad ruler, but then lots of times it to protect the resources that the government that is "helping" to protect the weak, is really doing it to still have access to the countries resources. I don't think its ever about really helping the innocent. If that was the case, why are there still people starving and not having a place to live, even in our own country?

Meditations
___

I really enjoyed practicing the art of meditation which I would do at different times of the day. In the end I prefer the single-focus meditation style.

When I first practiced this I would not be able to look at a focal point for very long before I needed to blink. As I did this more often I found I could look at a point of focus for quite a few minutes before blinking, then once I was tired I would shut my eyes for a few minutes and the repeat the exercise.

I found I really liked to do this in my car. I would drive to a quite place near our home at the river's edge and park. I would then focus on the tip of a branch and just stare at it and try to keep other thoughts from barging in. This is not a easy task to keeping other thoughts out, but when they do pop in, I refocus and not let the thought go any further.

I do notice that even though I am relaxed and focusing on the object, I am still aware of everything going on around me, I can hear sounds of traffic and birds singing, so I think this is normal, I am just not focusing on them.

I find this very relaxing and calming to me.

I feel as I do this more and more I will experience much more, which I am looking forward to.

I also do meditations with a relaxing music on my phone. I find this relaxing and the sounds help me to think of nothing else. But if I do this at bedtime I fall asleep. I see why its good to do meditation while sitting up for this very reason of getting relaxed too much and drifting off to sleep.

I tried chanting but this seems a little awkward to me, and will take more sessions to feel comfortable with it. The reason I do not do it too much is I seem to always do the single-focus meditation and not do the vocal one too often.

I think I can meditate at anytime even for a few minutes by just stopping when I am doing and closing my eyes and focusing on one sound. When I am working I do this, I shut my eyes, and all of a sudden I can hear the birds singing, which I did not notice while I was working. While my eyes are shut I only listen to that sound of singing and I do not think of anything else.
It is like a breath of fresh air to take these few minutes and do this.

Essay: Path of the Black Wizard

1. What are three interesting facts related to the Dark Arts that you've taken away from this class?

One of the interesting facts I have learned is that the study of the Dark Arts is about exploring the magical work and shedding light in the darkest corners, not creating darkness. That was a totally new way of looking at this, I always thought it was about evil when it is not. We study this class so that we can know what is out there and then know how to protect ourselves.

The second thing I learned is about the three basic areas of study, Defense Against the Dark Arts, Creatures of the Night and Low Magick.

I never heard of Low Magick not realizing it was also called Sorcery. Also that low magic is a tool and can be used for good or bad depending on the person doing it.

The third fact I learned was that I thought that all Sorcerers worshiped and did work for Satan, which they do not. Sorcerers try to control the powers of evil in a way to become divine themselves. And the difference between being a Wizard and a Sorcerer is that Wizards like to gain knowledge to gain wisdom and a Sorcerer wants to gain knowledge to use the power from it for selfish reasons.

2) Why are you interested in studying the Dark Arts?

I am interested in learning all the different departments of Wizardry being interested in all aspects of the classes offered. This was a choice of mine to touch base with all the departments and learn what I can from each one.

3) In your own words, describe what Sorcery/Low Magick is. What did you believe a Sorcerer was prior to reading this class material? Has what you learned in the lessons changed your mind?

I thought that Sorcery was completely bad, and never heard of the term Low Magick before this class. I found it interesting that you can practice Sorcery by keeping a moral balance of what you are doing. As the quote goes, "With great power comes great responsibility" this is something that must be adhered to if you are going to practice Sorcery in any form.

By making myself well rounded in wisdom and the different branches of magick I would be less apt to become imbalanced and place too much work in one area. You can use power but you need to use it with wisdom.

4) Before reading this class material, did you believe any of the misconceptions listed? Did something in this class material change an idea you held before?

I thought that the Dark Arts or a Black Wizard was always associated with evil. Learning that it is not was an eye-opener. I like how the class teaches us that yes, the Dark Arts do include studying things that can be harmful, but not any more then any other branch of Magick, or any mundane areas of study, I take Wortcunning classes and have learned about poisonous plants and how to use them for good or bad, its my choice how I use my wisdom. So I learned that being a Black Wizard does not mean you are evil.

Essay: The Story

The Story

To me the story makes me think of how it was before a person started to learn about being a wizard and then as they learn more about life, knowledge and more about themselves they become brighter and can share what they know with others. By doing this they are lighting the darkness around them. So before I started to learn I was in the dark, and I might have been the same as the person in the story walking around in a dark cave in total darkness and creepy swampy water at my feet.

Then as I learned more I could lighten up my way with the light of knowledge and even though I did not know much at first, I could still share it with others and in doing so brighten their lives too. Then as I shared my knowledge with others I got stronger myself by feeling better in helping others learn. In my studies I also met people who are smarter and brighter and have so much that they are willing to share with me, making me shine more brightly too.

For me this is so true, as I learn I feel capable of sharing things I know which in turns makes others learn too. And then they can share that knowledge and so on.

In my classes I tell everyone the new things I am learning, and we have great discussions on some of the topics. I think this is great. It brings a really good feeling in being able to do this.

It is interesting to realize that being a wizard is so much more about being wise then as we picture them in the movies. My daughter always says to people, my mother is a wizard, and I think they expect me to look like Gandolf, but its not like that. It's being the best you can be, and sharing it with others.

One of my examples of sharing what I know is what I learned in some herb classes, on growing my own Saffron. So now everyone I shared this with got the bulbs to plants, and now we can't wait to see them grow in the spring.

So my journey as becoming an apprentice wizard had become a light in the darkness that is so exciting to share and its nice to see people brighten up when they learn new things.

Essay: Black Wizard

1) Was the role of the Black Wizard what you thought it would be? If so, what was the most important part? If not, then how did the information change what you thought?

I thought at first that the role of the Black Wizard might be more in doing scary devious spells but to my surprise is it not so. I like how being a Black Wizard is more about learning all that there is to know good and evil and its up to the wizard himself or herself to do the art using their own personal moral code.

2) Did the "Sidewalk" lesson change the way you might think about things? Did it make sense? If yes, how? If no, why?

The "Sidewalk" lesson was great at teaching one to not take oneself too seriously. Which I think we all do and get offended if we think someone is laughing at us. As kids we tend to laugh more at people if they are different and act funny, not doing it out of being mean but because they are funny. So its good to remember if we are doing things other people might take it as comical rather then being mean, so its best to laugh at oneself too.
I like lesson of not taking oneself too seriously, and I try to do that anyhow. I have learned that when I make crafts or write a story, it's nice if other people like it, but it does not matters to me so much

anymore as long as I am happy with it. So if no one comments on something I have done, I now don't really care. (but sometimes that is easier said then done)

So its a less stressful way to live and the lessons in the "Sidewalk" hit the mark.

3) Morality/ Ethics Question:
You are really angry about a forum post that you read because it's bashing something that you really believe in. How do you respond? Why? Now that you've thought about it, what is another way you could approach it?

Ok, I don't really get angry over things that other people say, I might think to myself that I don't agree, but I don't get angry. If I was to respond I might ask they why they think that, so I could understand where there were coming from. Then if I still did not like it, I would usually say, well, that is interesting. And maybe say, back, "well what do you think of this," and ask them something in relationship to what they talked about, or what I thought it meant. This reminds me when I reposted a story about early Christians and the terrible things done in the name of God. One of my friends flipped out, and said I was Christian bashing. Which I thought was funny, but I responded to her, that it was not directed at her, and I was not bashing her, I was just reposting history.

4) After reading the lesson materials, do you feel Dark Arts an appropriate addition to your life path? If so, why? If you don't find the Dark Arts to be appropriate to your personal path, why not?

I think the Dark Arts will be a interesting subject to study and I plan on taking more classes to learn more.

I think one of the parts I liked learning was about it being a defense system. I think this is an important part of being a wizard, or for any wizard. It's like being a parent and knowing all the safeguards to protect your family and home.

Essay: Seeing The Waves: Your Magickal Journal

I chose a spiral bound journal with two colorful dragonflies on the cover.
It says: hope, dream, believe and imagine on the cover.

So I thought it was a fit journal to start with in talking about the synchronicities taking place
In my life.

I never thought of a journey by riding the ups and downs of a wave. It is quite interesting to
look and think about your life in that way. Riding the highs and lows of your life, but then trying to see in what direction you are headed by looking at the highs. It seems quite complicated in a way as you need to step back and really put some thought into it.

So I wrote about what was going on in my life with my pets. We love animals and have taken in rescues and the last one was our dog, who came all the way from Mississippi to Massachusetts. We also love cats, probably our favorite pets and have recently lost two of them and now we have three.

So the wave I have been riding this week has been the lows of the loss of our beloved pets, and the going up the wave to the top has been thinking that we could adopt a new cat and give one a good life, plus another kitty to love.

The wave on the top had been going from, being excited about the thought a new pet, and looking at pictures of animals that need to be adopted. Then doubting if we should get a new pet at all, and going down the wave thinking, well, everyone is at peace at home, all the animals get along and why disrupt the order of things.

Then thinking and getting exciting again riding the top, seeing the cute pets and even putting in a request to ask about a certain kitten. So I am still at the top with hopes of hearing back that The adoption will be accepted and picturing how everyone will be happy to welcome a new kitty into the family. Looking ahead at the best ways to introduce the new pet and how to set up the meetings with the others and planning its care and its future.

By seeing how happy I am at the top of the wave I know I am good with animals and love to take care of them. I have adopted in the past and will continue to give these animals a good home. It makes me happy to do this and this path will always be in my future.
I have written two books about a cat that I adopted a few years ago that was elderly and she was only with our family for a few months. (Tabitha and The Tabitha Tree) It was a choice I would never give up, as it was a spiritual journey for me to see the love and happiness that cat had before she died.

So riding the waves is a new exciting way for me to see what makes me happy and those feeling are what should guide me in the right paths to choose for my life.

Essay: Everyday Dangers

Mundane:
In my life I do not face any physical dangers, or have in the past. Over the past eighteen years I have faced the dangers of being overwhelmed with grief that could lead to depression, which in turn could lead to the use of antidepressants.
The cause of this was the lost of my 27 year old daughter in the Night Club Station Fire in 2003. That fire left one hundred people dead. Beside losing my daughter I raised her seven year old.

The way in which I dealt with this was at first very emotional and the use of prescription antidepressants. I was not happy with how I was feeling all the time and realized this was not a good thing. I looked at my granddaughter and knew she had to get through this and she was not being helped with any medications. When I realized this I stopped taking mine and got myself busy with her and life. Keeping busy with work and writing kept me focused. I chose to do the things my daughter wanted to do with her daughter and give her a good life. Even today, there are some hard times but mostly good.

Eventually I took classes in clay, the Grey School classes and played my piano and guitar. Doing things in life that made me feel good about myself. This is how I have got through this.

My daughter was into healing and she taught me about breathing and grounding. These things I would practice too. I learned more when I took classes about shielding and centering and this has been helpful to me also.

The Magickal things in my life that I have experience have been very interesting. I think I have ghosts in my home. We have had drops of water fall out of nowhere, the piano notes playing and door beads being moved, plus other odd things have gone on in our home and yard.

I deal with this by not being afraid and just knowing most likely whatever is going on is harmless. No one has ever been hurt. So I will acknowledge the presence and go on with my life.

What Happened The Year I Was Born

In 1952, the world was a different place.
There was no Google yet. Or Yahoo.
In 1952, the year of your birth, the top selling movie was This Is Cinerama. People buying the popcorn in the cinema lobby had glazing eyes when looking at the poster.

Remember, that was before there were DVDs. Heck, even before there was VHS. People were indeed watching movies in the cinema, and not downloading them online. Imagine the packed seats, the laughter, the excitement, the novelty. And mostly all of that without 3D computer effects.

Do you know who won the Oscars that year? The academy award for the best movie went to The Greatest Show on Earth. The Oscar for best foreign movie that year went to Forbidden Games. The top actor was Gary Cooper for his role as Marshal Will Kane in High Noon. The top actress was Shirley Booth for her role as Lola Delaney in Come Back, Little Sheba. The best director? John Ford for The Quiet Man.

In the year 1952, the time when you arrived on this planet, books were still popularly read on paper, not on digital devices. Trees were felled to get the word out. The number one US bestseller of the time was The Silver Chalice by Thomas B. Costain. Oh, that's many years ago. Have you read that book? Have you heard of it?

In 1952... West Germany has 8 million refugees inside its borders. Elizabeth II is proclaimed Queen of the United Kingdom at St. James's Palace, London, England. In the Hague Tribunal, Israel demands reparations worth $3 billion from Germany. The Treaty of Taipei is signed between Japan and the Republic of China to officially end the Second Sino-Japanese War. The Diary of Anne Frank is published. The United States Army Special Forces is created. A British passenger jet flies twice over the Atlantic Ocean in the same day. Martial law is declared in Kenya due to the Mau Mau uprising. The first successful surgical separation of Siamese twins is conducted in Mount Sinai Hospital, Cleveland, Ohio.

That was the world you were born into. Since then, you and others have changed it.

The Nobel prize for Literature that year went to François Mauriac. The Nobel Peace prize went to Albert Schweitzer. The Nobel prize for physics went to Felix Bloch and Edward Mills Purcell from the

United States for their development of new methods for nuclear magnetic precision measurements and discoveries in connection therewith. The sensation this created was big. But it didn't stop the planets from spinning, on and on, year by year. Years in which you would grow bigger, older, smarter, and, if you were lucky, sometimes wiser. Years in which you also lost some things. Possessions got misplaced. Memories faded. Friends parted ways. The best friends, you tried to hold on. This is what counts in life, isn't it?

The 1950s were indeed a special decade. The American economy is on the upswing. The cold war between the US and the Soviet Union is playing out throughout the whole decade. Anti-communism prevails in the United States and leads to the Red Scare and accompanying Congressional hearings. Africa begins to become decolonized. The Korean war takes place. The Vietnam War starts. The Suez Crisis war is fought on Egyptian territory. Fidel Castro, Che Guevara and others overthrow authorities to create a communist government on Cuba. Funded by the US, reconstructions in Japan continue. In Japan, film maker Akira Kurosawa creates the movies Rashomon and Seven Samurai. The FIFA World Cups are won by Uruguay, then West Germany, then Brazil.

Do you remember the movie that was all the rage when you were 15? In the Heat of the Night. Do you still remember the songs playing on the radio when you were 15? Maybe it was Ode to Billie Joe by Bobbie Gentry. Were you in love? Who were you in love with, do you remember?

In 1952, 15 years earlier, a long time ago, the year when you were born, the song Wheel of Fortune by Kay Starr topped the US charts. Do you know the lyrics? Do you know the tune? Sing along.

The wheel of fortune
Goes spinning around
Will the arrow point my way?
Will this be my day?

...

There's a kid outside, shouting, playing. It doesn't care about time. It doesn't know about time. It shouts and it plays and thinks time is forever. You were once that kid.

When you were 9, the movie Hercules in the Haunted World was playing. When you were 8, there was Pollyanna.

6, 5, 4, 3, 2, 1... it's 1952. There's TV noise coming from the second floor. Someone turned up the volume way too high. The sun is burning from above. These were different times. The show playing on TV is Kukla, Fran and Ollie. The sun goes down. Someone switches channels. There's The Ed Sullivan Show on now. That's the world you were born in.

Progress, year after year. Do you wonder where the world is heading towards? The technology available today would have blown your mind in 1952. Do you know what was invented in the year you were born? Diet soft drinks. Optical Fiber. The Fusion Bomb.

I work here nights parking cars
Underneath the moon and the stars
Same ones that we all knew
Back in 1952

...

That's from the song 3rd Base, Dodger Stadium by Ry Cooder.
In 1952, a new character entered the world of comic books: Astro Boy. Bang! Boom! But that's just fiction, right? In the real world, in 1952, Christopher Reeve was born. And Dan Aykroyd. Douglas

Adams, too. And you, of course. Everyone an individual. Everyone special. Everyone taking a different path through life.
It's 2019.
The world is a different place.
What path have you taken?
(from www.mybirthdayfacts.com)

Essay: Vampires and Werewolves

I would think that psychic vampires who feed on ambient energy would spend most of their time in places such as night clubs, busy cities such as New York, Los Angeles and New Orleans where people tend to be up all night expending their energies on all sorts of activities.
It would be a perfect place for psychic vampires to dwell.
I would think they would avoid the boring places in life such as libraries and old age homes where not much energy is flowing freely.
If I was going to be a were-creature I would be a were-wolf.
I think a were-wolf would be a great life to be as this sort of creature. I could change and run free and fast though the woods. I would be strong and able to defend myself. Even though a were-raptor would be strong and if someone saw it they would freak out whereas a wolf might be taken as more normal to see.
Being a were-raven would be awesome as to the flying ability, but I don't think they would be so great at attacking someone and not be noticed as their life is mostly spent in the daytime hours and not night.

The Were-wolf would be able to hunt and attack at night and not be noticed, until someone found the remains of what it killed.

I had a dream and this is how I became a were-wolf. I was captured by a woman who was a were-wolf and she took me to this room. I was sitting on a bed telling her the many reasons why I should not be bitten and made into a were-wolf but she did not listen.

Soon I was bitten and turned into a were-wolf, and found myself sitting at a table with her eating chicken. She had a nice set of clothes on but I did not have any yet. I was bigger then her and would learn how to be a werewolf from her.

The room we were in was in a basement of a shopping mall. Soon we pulled away a chest of drawer from against the wall and behind that was a stairway that led up to the mall.

We went up there and killed everyone we could find.

That was the beginning of my life as a were-wolf.

My Personal Altar

Before I got a table for my altar, I pictured one about 3 feet high that would fit just right into my bedroom. I wanted something not too big but not too small, I had an area picked out for it.
So my usual way of finding something I need is that I always put it out to the universe that I am looking for whatever I need. Then in a short time it always seems to show up.
So I did this and went on my daily routine of going to the bank and post office and then I stopped at one used items store. I check in there and nothing seemed to fit what I actually wanted. The tables were a little too big, or sort of ugly and not just what I wanted, but I almost bought one just so I could set up my altar that very day, but changed my mind and did not buy the ugly little table.
Then I went to the grocery store and stopped by another used clothing store that sells books. This is the store that I buy my books that I resell. So I got my bag of books and as I was leaving and walking out the door, over behind a clothes rack up on a shelf, covered with knick knacks was my table! So I asked if that table was display only or would they sell it. A few minutes later I was walking out the door with my perfect table.
It was painted a pretty yellow with little leaves painted in green around the edges. This represented to me my Wortcunning classes that I take. It also has a middle shelf and a drawer.

Now that I have it home, I put on a tie dyed pretty cloth that my daughter made as the alter cover. It is in pretty blues and pinks. So I can think of her when I look at it. When I stand in front of the alter it faces between east and west.

In the middle shelf I put three dishes of my collection of rocks, gems and crystals.

For the top I but a geode to represent the earth. A scallop shell to represent water. I put a marble cat to remind me of my love of animals. I put a meditation bell and a cat yoga statue to remind me of my daughter Lisa Jean who has passed. I tap the bell before I do anything as putting forth my intentions for the day. I have a incense burner to represent fire.

On the wall behind my altar I hung a mirror that also has a small candle in front of it. I can see my reflection in it when I stand in front of my altar. This mirror to to represent the divine spirit.

I also have on my altar my Athame which the handle is carved like a dragon to represent my chosen name. And I also have a crystal wand and a small crystal ball. I also have three candles that I can light. I also have sage that I like to burn when I do any intentions.

In the middle drawer I keep my cones of incense and matches and extra sage.

Once I set it up I did do the Rite of Consecration.

So far I have used my alter three times. The first was the Rite of Consecration. Then I did another day when I said my intentions, and used sage to remove any negative energies and to set the intention of being a helpful person that will listen to others talk and not interrupt them. Yesterday I did my intentions again and also did the sage ritual to my husband asking to protect him, keep him safe, and to increase his creativity.

I really love having the altar, it gives me a time in the day to stop being active to stand back and think what my intentions should be to improve and help others. To take a breath and realize there is not a big hurry, to think and realize what is important for that day.

Since then I have set up a new altar which I like more as I could add a shelf with items that have many memories.

Essay: Being Prepared

My plan of action to protect myself from malevolent forces or just plain negative people, or the stress of the world around me includes a few daily rituals that I try to practice everyday.
 One of the things I like to do is to sage my home and say as I do this for all negative energies to leave and to have this a happy home. I also will sage myself and I do this once or twice per month. This does make my living space feel so much more positive.

I practice centering and I also do a protective circle around myself. If I am around people who are negative or I feel they are trying to argue to prove a point, I will take a deep breath a few times and release it. I always try to use my common sense and avoid a argument just to prove a point. Most times I will just say, well, that is a interesting point of view. I will think about that, thanks. It seems everyone thinks its so important that their point of view is correct when its not that important at all, so its never worth getting into a heated argument. Just take a deep breathe if you have to and walk away.

This breathing also helps when life just gets stressful with a busy schedule. Just shutting your eyes, breathing and putting up your protective shield can make a world of difference.

I feel that the exercises I have learned as far as centering and the protective shields, all work well for magikal and mundane issues that come up in my life.

I also maintain a healthy diet.

I am always aware of my surrounding wherever I go.
These are all common sense things to do to keep yourself safe.

I find that these practices and all the lessons I have learned have helped keep myself a stable and reasonable person.

Essay: The Path Ahead

My interests in life have been leading me towards this path of study for years. As a child I was full of questions and collected rocks, bugs, bones, and kept them organized on shelfs and the bones and dead insects I would keep preserved in alcohol in a jar.
It was not until I was older that I came across the Grey School of Wizardry. I found it fascinating that so many subjects were offered for study. I immediately signed up, excited to be able to learn on my own with great professors.
I took quite a few classes and then got busy in life and stopped.
I just recently restarted, but sadly to say all my work and class test results could not be found.
So I am doing some over and taking some new ones.

As I look ahead I have been excited to have the time to do this again and increase my knowledge of wizardry things. In my excitement I have shared this with my family and two family members just signed up to do classes.

What I love about this is learning. I have taken a few classes in Wortcunning and the knowledge I have learned I use almost everyday. I also tell others about what they can you with herbs to improve their lives to to use in cooking.

As a mother and grandmother we are always in the role of teaching our children and I have a business that works with inmates and I am always giving out helpful advise to my inmates when asked for help. When this happens the advise I give just seem to flow from me to them.
So the more I learn the more I can share and help other people.

I also have always felt like I was something like a witch, but not, I like to do things on my own and being a wizard seems to fill the spot for me.
Also at our local Wicca plant nursery the owner did a reading for me, told me that I was always a wizard. That really took me by surprise as she did not know me well.

I am looking forward to leaning more and more and can't wait to do my studies. I am a little anxious at times about the assignments, sometimes it seems like so much work, but I take it a little at a time.

I like to print out my material for lessons and keep all the information in a notebook for each class that I can keep as a reference if I need to look up things I might forget.

It will be nice to be able to know enough to progress to being a better wizard and to help others in life and with problems or questions that I will be capable of answering.

In my life right now I write children's books, make painted stained glass, hand crafted clay dragons and plant containers, necklaces. I paint and know how to hook rugs and crochet. I also know how to raise chickens, tend honey bees, take care of farm animals and pets such as cats and dogs, fish, lizards and spiders. Sewing, cooking and may other things that I already know that I am glad to share the how to with anyone that wants to know. I feel like I am on the right path and wish I started this journey when I was younger. At this point in my life I am ready to ride the wave!

A Meditation To Pass The Time

To help you pass the time I am going to teach you how to do a meditation. You can go anyplace you want in the world by doing this. But I will teach you a basic one.
So, relax and lay down or do it anywhere at all.
Shut your eyes, and go back to a time say when you were a little kid. I want you to picture these places in your mind. And only go back to good times, not bad.
Ok, so picture yourself standing outside your door to your house. Picture everything you can remember about it and then walk in.

Look at the first room. Look at everything and remember how it looked. Then go to the next room, do this in your whole house. You might even picture people there doing things. Take your time. You will remember more things then you thought you would. Go to your own room, and look at all your stuff. Then go back outside when you are done and look around. Practice this, and you will get to remember lots you forgot. I love doing this one, and going home to see it again.

It will be like you are there. Now you can do that at any place you have ever been.

You can also make up new places, picture yourself going to the woods, and seeing the trees, see how tall they are, is it winter or summer, look at the ground and see the plants and bugs, just travel in your mind. It's a great trip. You can be anywhere you want.

So actually you are there, your spirit is there looking at these things. Enjoy .

Essay: Who Are You?

I am the person that I want to be. I am myself all of the time and I am content with who I am. I like the way I can pick up new things to learn and I am always imaginative and having fun with life. I think I am the way I am on purpose. Life, influences from parents, friends, pets, have molded me into the person I am. Depending on my life, the experiences I have had would make me either this way or that. We make our choices in life, but the past makes and affects our present personalities.

Right now I feel I am mature with much more wisdom then I had in my twenties. But I still feel the excitement life offers. I love my animals and all the hobbies I enjoy. I have so many interests I find it hard to keep up. If I was to change I would like to find more space for myself, more relaxing times and to enjoy things at a slower pace and also to be more creative, wiser and understanding. I would like to be a better vegetarian, I am in the process an find it hard to always do but I am working on it.

I try to live by these five principles:

One is the I stand for my beliefs. I will stand up and have my say for what I think is right, I am very stubborn and will not back down unless you can logically show me a different way. Another principle is that I will show courage against opposition, even though it is hard for me to do, I will be nervous and even try to get out of it, but when it comes down to the line, I will stand up and have my say. Thirdly, I will always oppose evil, in all shapes an forms. I don't think I have personally confronted "evil" but I know evil goes completely against my inner self. The fourth rule is that I believe in speaking the truth, and keeping my word. It is so much easier to speak the truth then to try to cover up lies. I keep my word and if I cannot I will stand up and say so. One of the ways I am proud of keeping my word is when my daughter died, I got court permission to see my granddaughter every Wednesday and on the weekends. I have never missed a Wednesday or weekend to see her, no matter what, I was there rain, snow, sick or tired except for one time I could not get there because of a blizzard. I was driving there to get her, and my windshield wiper broke on the highway, I could not see to drive, I crept off the next exit looking out the window and got it fixed and the snow was so bad I went home. I got her the next day.

She depended on me and I kept that promise to her.

The last principle is that I like to be generous. I find this is so easy to do, and makes so many happy, it feels good and helps out others. I believe what you give comes back to you. I don't give for this reason, but because it makes me feel happy that I am able to share good things with others.

Essay: Definition of a Green Wizard

Since I was a child I always loved gardening. My parents had a field of vegetables and even when I was little I would help weed the rows. I also helped plant all the vegetable seeds, and I can recognize each seed even today of what plant it will grow into.
I loved the little carrot seeds and the bumpy spiked beet seeds. I remember placing them one by one a little bit apart. It took a long time to plant a row.
I was also taught how to make the holes to plant tomatoes and cabbage and peppers. And how to put a strip of paper around each plant so the snails and bugs would not crawl up and eat them. I loved making the big round circles in the ground for the squash seeds. We would did a large circle out about 4 inches deep and layer it with cow manure, then a layer of soil then the seeds. In the fall I would help prepare the baskets of vegetables for canning.
I loved running in the garden in my bare feet. It was always a big part of my childhood.
My mom even gave me my own flower garden that I tended. Plus I was taught all the flower and tree names.

So I think being a green witch has always been in my blood. As I got older me and my friends loved to drink herb teas and cook with all sorts of spices and herbs.

Now at this point in my life when I came across this class I thought this is great, now I can really learn about plants and herbs and how to use them in many ways.
I would like to be able to know more about how herbs effect our bodies and minds. To know which ones are best to help us feel better.
I also would like to grow my own herb garden and not like the usually way of just having them, but to really know about each plant and its benefits and dangers.

I was surprised when I was told that you can eat tomatoes but not the leaves the same with rhubarb. My brother taught me to eat dandelion leaves in the spring and we picked the flowers to make wine. It was all so interesting.

I have taken a few classes already and have learned how to pick lavender and the proper way to dry and store it. This was important to me as I have now dried other herbs and have them on my kitchen shelf. I think being a green witch is learning to use the plants we have and to use them in a way that is important to us either in cooking, healing or gardening.
To me all the knowledge is there to learn. We can then share what we learn with others and teach our children how to do these things.

To me being a kitchen witch or green wizard is exciting and fun almost like being a scientist.
I can't wait to learn more.

LETS EAT THIS CREATURE

THIS IS A STORY OF TWO DRAGON FRIENDS. THEY WERE MORE THEN JUST FRIENDS THEY WERE THE BEST OF FRIENDS. THEY SHOULD HAVE BEEN BORN TWINS THEY WERE SO CLOSE.
THEY MET WHEN THEY WERE LITTLE AND WERE HATCHED NEXT TO EACH OTHER IN THE CAVE ON ONE OF THE TALLEST MOUNTAINS IN THE WORLD.
AS SOON AS THEY HATCHED THEY CRAWLED TO EACH OTHER AND LOOKED EACH OTHER IN THE EYES AND WERE FROM THAT MOMENT ON BONDED TOGETHER LIKE REAL BROTHERS.
THE MOTHER DRAGONS WERE BEST FRIENDS TOO, SO MAYBE THAT HAD SOMETHING TO DO WITH IT.

THE MOUNTAIN THEY LIVED ON WAS VERY FAR AWAY FROM EVERYONE, THE MOUNTAIN ITSELF WAS SURROUNDED BY OTHER MOUNTAINS. EVEN IF YOU TRIED TO FIND IT, IT WOULD BE ALMOST IMPOSSIBLE.

IT WAS EASY FOR DRAGONS TO GET THERE AS THEY COULD FLY BUT IF YOU WALKED YOU WOULD GET LOST FOR SURE.

AS THE DRAGONS GOT A LITTLE OLDER THEY WERE ALLOWED TO GO OUTSIDE THE CAVE AND PLAY. THEY WERE NOT OLD ENOUGH TO FLY AND HAD TO STAY NEAR THEIR MOTHERS.
THE MOTHER DRAGONS TOOK TURNS FLYING OFF TO FIND FOOD FOR THEIR YOUNG.
THEY WOULD BRING BACK WHATEVER THEY CAUGHT LIKE FISH, TOADS, BIRDS, SQUIRRELS, AND WHEN THE HUNTING GOT BAD BUGS!

SOMETIMES THE MOTHER DRAGONS WOULD TAKE THESE TWO LITTLE DRAGONS OUT INTO THE WOODS TO WALK AND TEACH THEM ABOUT LIFE AND HOW TO FIND FOOD AND THE DANGERS TO BE AWARE OF.

THE MOTHER DRAGONS TOOK THE TWO TO A BIG LAKE AND TAUGHT THEM HOW TO SWIM. MOST DRAGONS DO NOT LIKE TO SWIM BUT IT IS IMPORTANT TO KNOW HOW TO JUST IN CASE. THE LITTLE DRAGONS DID NOT WANT TO GO INTO THE WATER, THEY WERE AFRAID AND SAID : "NO, IT WAS TOO COLD AND SCARY,"
BUT THE MOHTER DRAGONS SAID, WELL SOMEDAY YOU MIGHT NEED TO KNOW HOW TO SWIM. WHAT IF YOU WERE FLYING OVER THE LAKE AND SOMETHING HAPPENED TO YOUR WINGS AND YOU FELL OUT OF THE SKY RIGHT INTO THE WATER? WHAT WOULD YOU DO? YOU CAN'T LET YOURSELF DROWN, SO YOU NEED TO KNOW THIS LIFE SAVING SKILL.
THE YOUNG DRAGONS PUT IN ONE FOOT AND THEN THE OTHER AND SOON WERE NECK HIGH IN THE WATER. SOON THEY WERE LAUGHING AND NOT AFRIAD AT ALL, AS A MATTER OF FACT THEY SORT OF LIKED IT.

ANOTHER SKILL THEY HAD TO LEARN WAS HOW TO FIND BUGS TO EAT.

THEY DID NOT LIKE TO EAT BUGS BUT THE MOTHERS TOLD THEM, THAT IF THEY CAN'T FIND FOOD THEY HAVE TO EAT OR STARVE. IT WAS BETTER TO EAT BUGS THEN STARVE.

SO THEY WERE TAUGHT HOW TO TURN OVER LOGS AND LOOK UNDER THEM FOR BUGS AND SOMETIMES EVEN A LIZARD WOULD BE LURKING UNDER IT. DRAGONS DID LIKE TO EAT LIZARDS. IT WAS A SMALL SNACK BUT IN HARD TIMES IT TOOK OFF THE HUNGRY WILLIES YOU GET WHEN ITS TIME TO EAT. THEY ALSO LEARNED HOW TO LOOK CLOSELY AT THE BARK OF A TREE, THERE YOU WILL FIND MOTHS HIDING UNTIL THE NIGHT DRAWS THEM OUT, OR ANTS CRAWLING UP AND DOWN.

ANOTHER GOOD PLACE TO FIND BUGS WAS UNDER ROCKS. THE DRAGONS COULD MOVE BIG BOULDERS AND ONE DAY EVEN CAUSED A ROCKSLIDE DOWN THE EDGE OF THE MOUNTAIN. WHEN THEY PUSHED A BOULDER IT WENT RIGHT DOWN THE SIDES KNOCKING OVER TREES AND CAUSING OTHER BOULDERS TO FOLLOW.

AFTER THE DUST SETTLED THE ROCKSLIDE LEFT A BIG DIRT PATH DOWN THE SIDE OF THE MOUNTAIN, THE DRAGONS WERE SOON ALL SLIDING DOWN AND HAVE SO MUCH FUN.

THE MOTHER DRAGONS WERE YELLING DOWN AT THEM, "HAVE FUN WALKING BACK, YOUR WINGS ARE NOT READY YET TO FLY! "

THE DRAGONS THAT LIVED ON THIS MOUNTAIN COULD DO WHATEVER THEY WANTED, THEY WERE SO FAR FROM CIVILIZATION THAT NO ONE KNEW THEY LIVED THERE.
AS FAR AS HUMANS WERE CONCERNED DRAGONS WERE LONG GONE. HUMANS ONLY READ STORIES ABOUT THEM IN OLD BOOKS AND SOME DID NOT EVEN BELIEVE THEY EXISTED.
IMAGINE THAT!

AS THE DRAGONS GREW THEY GOT TO GO OUT AND EXPLORE ON THERE OWN MORE AND MORE AND HUNTED AND FOUND FOOD FOR EACH OTHER AND THEIR MOTHERS.
SOON THEIR WINGS GOT STRONG AND THEY STARTED TO RUN AND JUMP AND TAKE OFF FROM THE GROUND A FEW FEET AT A TIME. SOON ENOUGH THEY WERE FLYING OVER THE SHORT BUSHES AND A FEW WEEKS LATER THEY WERE SOARING OVER THE TREETOPS.

FROM WAY UP HIGH THEY COULD SEE FOR MILES AND MILES BUT NEVER ONCE DID THEY SEE ANY PEOPLE. THEIR MOTHERS TOLD THEM ABOUT PEOPLE AND WHAT THEY WERE LIKE, BUT NEVER DID THEY SEE ANY. THEY ONLY KNEW ABOUT THEM FROM STORIES THE OLDEST DRAGONS TOLD. THE STORIES OF THE OLD DAYS WHEN THERE WERE KINGS AND QUEENS AND DRAGON HUNTERS, BUT THAT WAS HUNDREDS OF YEARS AGO AND PEOPLE HAD FORGOTTEN ALL ABOUT THEM. SO THERE WAS NO NEED TO WORRY. JUST STAY IN OUR MOUNTAINS AND WE ARE SAFE.

SO LIFE WENT ON AND THE TWO BEST FRIENDS DID EVERYTHING TOGETHER , THEY NEVER ARGUED AND GOT ALONG JUST FINE UNTIL ONE DAY SOMETHING STRANGE HAPPENED.

THE DRAGONS HAD FLOWN FARTHER THEN THEY EVER HAD BEFORE IN THIER LIFE, THEY WERE JUST FLYING AND FLYING AND FORGOT WHERE THEY WERE, SOON THEY REALIZED THERE WERE NO MORE MOUNTAINS.

THEY WERE IN SHOCK, AND THEY SAW FLAT LAND AND A STRANGE LOOKING CREATURE THAT LOOKED LIKE A WOLF BUT WAS NOT. IT WAS RUNNING IN A FIELD BELOW THEM AND THEY WERE SO CURIOUS THEY JUST HAD TO LAND AND TAKE A LOOK

SO THEY LANDED AND TRIED TO HIDE BEHIND SOME TREES BUT THE CREATURE SAW THEM AND STARTED TO BARK AND BARK AND BARK.

THE DRAGONS DID NOT KNOW WHAT DO DO, SO ONE OF THEM RAN OUT FAST AND SCOOPED UP THE WOLF LIKE CREATURE AND FLEW RIGHT UP INTO THE AIR, THE OTHER DRAGON FOLLOWED BEHIND AND THEY BOTH FLEW AS FAST AS THE WIND AND WENT HOME TO TELL THEIR MOTHERS WHAT THEY FOUND.

WELL AS SOON AS THEY LANDED, THEY FOUND A NOTE SAYING THE MOTHERS HAD GONE OFF FOR A WEEK ON A BIG HUNT.

THE TWO DRAGONS JUST LOOKED AT EACH OTHER AND THEN AT THE CREATURE THEY FOUND.
THE CREATURE WAS VERY SCARED AND JUST SAT ON THE GROUND TREMBLING AND LOOKING AT THEM WITH BIG SAD BROWN EYES. IT WAS WHITE WITH BLACK SPOTS AND HAD LITTLE EARS AND A CUTE BLACK NOSE.

ONE DRAGON FELT A LITTLE SAD THAT HE TOOK THE CREATURE FROM HIS HOME AND DID NOT KNOW WHAT TO DO, SO HE MADE LITTLE COOING SOUNDS AT IT AND PICKED IT UP AND CUDDLED IT. AS SOON AS HE DID THAT, THE LITTLE WOLF LIKE CREATURE, LICKED THE DRAGON RIGHT ON HIS CHEEK!
THAT ONE GESTURE MELTED HIS HEART ON THE SPOT, BUT THE OTHER DRAGON WAS EYEING THE WOLF LIKE CREATURE AND LICKING HIS CHOPS.

SO HE SAID, "LETS EAT THE WOLF LIKE CREATURE, I AM SURE IT IS GOOD"

AND THE OTHER DRAGON WHO NEVER ONCE IN HIS LIFE DISAGREED WITH HIS BEST FRIEND SAID, "OK, BUT NO, WE CAN'T LOOK AT IT, ITS SO CUTE."

"BUT ITS FOOD AND I AM HUNGRY AFTER THAT LONG FLIGHT" SAID THE OTHER DRAGON.

AND THE DRAGON HOLDING THE WOLF LIKE CREATURE SAID, "I KNOW, BUT ITS SO CUDDLY AND WARM AND IT LIKES ME."

"BUT WHAT ARE WE GOING TO TELL OUR MOTHERS, LIKE WHERE WE FOUND IT WAS OFF LIMITS, WE WOULD BE IN SO MUCH TROUBLE, IT WOULD BE MUCH EASIER TO EAT IT AND HIDE THE EVIDENCE." SAID THE OTHER DRAGON.

AND THE DRAGON HOLDING THE WOLF LIKE CREATURE SAID, "WE CAN HIDE IT IN THE WOODS AND IT CAN BE OUR FRIEND AND WE CAN PLAY WITH IT."

"OH, JUST STOP IT, LETS JUST EAT THE WOLF LIKE CREATURE. " SAID THE OTHER DRAGON AND HE WAS GETTING REALLY STEAMING MAD.

AND THE OTHER DRAGON WITH THE WOLF LIKE CREATURE JUST UP AND FLEW AWAY HOLDING THE WOLF LIKE CREATURE IN ITS TALONS.
HE FLEW AND FLEW AND HID IN ANOTHER CAVE ON THE OTHER SIDE OF THE MOUNTAIN AND THERE HE STAYED WITH HIS NEW FRIEND. HE COULD NOT BEAR TO EAT THIS AMAZING SOFT CREATURE, WHO LOOKED AT HIM WITH BIG BROWN EYES THAT JUST MELTED HIS HEART. HE DID NOT KNOW WHAT TO DO, BUT EAT THIS, HE COULD NOT, HIS BIG DRAGON HEART WOULD NOT LET HIM.

HIS BEST FRIEND WOULD JUST HAVE TO UNDERSTAND.

SO WHICH DRAGON WOULD YOU HAVE BEEN? THE ONE WHO SAVED THE WOLF LIKE CREATURE OR WOULD YOU HAVE EATEN IT?

(this story is going to be a children's book)

Essay: Jade Plant

The Jade plant is a succulent from the family Crassula, C.Ovata, C. Argentea and C.Portulaca. Many people call it a money plant or dollar plant and bring it as a housewarming gift.

The plants appearance is that is the leaves grow on a stocky stem that that branches out, the leaves are oval and thick. The leaves grow two per section and alternate as it grows on the stems.
It has no smell but will produce white fragrant flowers certain times of the year.

From sitting and looking at my Jade plant I have written my Doctrine of Signatures:

The leaves are thick and fleshy possibly contains a fluid that could be used to treat the skin an wounds like the Aloe plant.
The Stems are thick and seem to put on a hard shield as it gets older. Being strong like this it could contain fiber that would be good for digestion.
The plant is pleasant to look at, with a calming green color, so it would be a nice plant to have in a house to make you feel relaxed.

True Medical uses of this plant:
This plant has been used to treat nausea in Africa and is used also to treat epilepsy, diarrhea, and corns. In China a variety with pointed leaves is used to treat diabetic systems.
To use it they boil the leaves and use the liquids.

In a folk remedy to treat warts, the leaf is cut open the the moist fleshy part of it is placed over a wart for a few days. If it is successful the wart will fall off.
It is also used to treat cuts and sores and to relieve pain. To do this the leaves are cut in half and put over the sore, then a plaster on top of that.

This plant is used for food for the Khoi and Africans. They use the roots by grating and cooking them eating it with thick milk. Maybe this is like a pudding.
The Feng Shui believe that the Jade plants have calming effect.

References:
Wiki
Worldofsucculents.com

Reiki reading with Shari

I will write down things as I remember them.

She said, everyone was there like talking around a table.

Lisa, Derek, Shawn, Dennis, Mom, Mrs. Kelly, Greg Sewell, Bobby Sewell. Grandma Bolton.

Someone's birthday, (Lisa) she is shoving a cake in her face..
I buy one every year for her birthday, and I think everyone thinks its weird, but she said that Lisa likes it, so to keep doing it.

Also Lisa shows her me rolling out dough, we think its for the apple squares more than, pie.
She says to make it, as she wants to taste it through me.

Lisa said to eat more. Also to make the soup, with lots of different textures in it.

(So today I made a nice beef stew with green beans, carrots, potatoes, onions, beef and parsley :-)

She talked about a older woman who died with congestive heart failure, (my mom, died of this) she was standing next to a taller

thinner woman, who sang (Mrs. Kelly)
and does someone play the piano? of course I do, or did, and I think it was Bobo, as she was saying something about her music she wants me to play, we could not figure out the song. So saying I should play it more. (Bobo was the nickname for my grandmother)

Lisa and Dennis they take care of each other. It showed it was her dad, or step dad, which he was.

There was a Colorado connection, all I can think of was Derek. She said he took his own life, was depressed and not his fault, as he was under a chemical influence. He had a hard time being here.

Shawn was not in the front at all, but more in the background, but did show up as a younger brother to Lisa, and shorter than Derek, and Derek showed up with darker hair than Shawn.

Lisa she said was very independent.

Lisa showed her the last thing she saw before she died, was her arm like pulling on someone, to help them. She felt her near the door, but it was blocked.

Lisa said that was it, she did not remember anything else, she said something like that was all the shit she remembered at the very end.

Also I said I told lisa that she better be there when I die, and Shari told me even if she did come back, her higher self would be there.

But Lisa told me, no problem Mom. So I know I will see her when I die.

A man was there who died suddenly of an aneurysm, so I said that was Bobby. My brother in-law.

I wanted to know more about Greg Sewell. She said he had eyes that you noticed, and was good hearted, and liked people. He knew how to make you feel good with him.

On the fire, she said stairs and upstairs. She thought the fire started near the stairs which it did in the fireplace.

Greg did not want to really talk about it, he did not care about it anymore.

So I asked if she can find out more about what happened.

She saw a dog, but not two, she thought one died first from the smoke, but after I told her there were two, she said the one that was lighter or more golden than the one that died first was trying to wake up greg.

She said, the smoke was light at that time, and you know when your asleep and have to pee, and you like don't wake up but know you have to wake up and go pee, well he was in that state of mind, where he knew he had to get up, but could not. Probably because of the smoke. She did not see coughing or anything like that.

On the reiki healing, she asked if I had diabetes, but I do not, as she felt poor circulation in my feet, and said sometimes people with that, have that. But said it could be I need to ground into the earth and take in energy.

That I hold in peoples problems and do not release them, so it makes me split like, so I like to help people, but also makes me anti- social as its too much.
And that's because I do not let it go.
And I am learning better, even before I went to her to do this. (I have been working on that myself, as with others, to let them solve their own problems and to stay out of their business.) I try to back off so this is a good thing, But as she was healing me I could feel over my stomach area, where her hands were, she was pulling her hand away quite a few times, and I could actually feel like her pulling something from me, like say she was pulling a rope out of me,

it was weird, and I asked her what it was, she said she was taking out all the things I was holding in.
She was surprised I could feel it so much.
She also did something to my right knee and I could feel that.

Lisa also showed her a long type building, like a hotel maybe, with a wrap around porch, white, also had balcony, she was looking down on it, but when I see it I might be looking up at it. I am suppose to pay attention to it when I see it. (we went to New Hampshire, and saw the Mount Washington Hotel, this must be the place Lisa wanted me to see, its so awesome)

She said I should dance, do whatever, have fun. To do what ever makes me feel connected. The drum would be good for me. Like the deep Native American type drum.

When we were done, I was quite light headed and sat for a little bit. As I sat their Shari did something to my legs and feet, I think she was grounding me.

She also saw a horse, a full grown horse, and she said he was working with me too.
The only horse I had was Captain.

She was shown a four leaf clover? Lisa liked the Irish, being a Kelly, maybe that is why.
Lisa also thanked me for taking care of Zoe Jean, and letting Zoe Jean be herself.

Now at home, I feel so much better about myself. Lighter, and that I am not so weird.
We talked about the alien connection, and the my vision of mars. And also about the dream of Lisa coming to me and giving me a kiss on the lips and seeing her smiling face.

On myself, when she first started she told me I have always been a Shaman, a death walker and strong healer. Always in all of my past lives.

A Shaman can also be a Wizard,

I looked up the definition:
"A Shaman is an intermediary between this world and the spirit world. They act on behalf of the community; conducting ceremonial ritual healing the people, and helping to guide others on the shamanic path. A shamans life belongs to the village and it is their responsibility to ensure the wellbeing of the family, the community an all of creation.
In this way the shaman helps to maintain balance and harmony on both a personal and planetary level."

A few years ago when I went to Seven Arrows, she did a reading, and one of the things she said, was I was that I was always a wizard. And she knew nothing of my interests in it.

People and your art

I seem to find that most people are so weird when it comes to things that you might like to do, or projects, and when you share them say on facebook or by email, you do not get any response, this goes for family too. Its so weird.
When people show me something they have done, I am always interested looking at the painting, book, or project. I talk about it, and what I liked.
I am always impressed by the things people create.

You can talk to a person and not know much about them, but then you get to see things they do, like cooking, gardening, painting, writing or whatever, and its such a pleasure to see what they create. I am always excited.
But then I post something that I have done, and hardly anyone responds, not even a like. Most of time not even one click. But I can post a stupid joke or a cat and get tons of replies or posts.

Its like pulling teeth to get people to express anything if its not about themselves. Its very disappointing. I even had a party for a book I got published, the party was for the people who donated a recipe for the book, and I got them all a copy of it. It was a great party, but then family were also invited that had nothing to do with the book, but do you think they would have said anything at all to me about it, or ask to see it, or even look at the other books I had laid out for people to check out? No not a word. What is that about?

But they are the first ones to talk about something they did, and they want you to listen to everything they tell you about how it went making it and so on and so on, and how fucking smart they want to seem to be.
And of course, I listen and tell then how awesome it is, and that I want to see it or buy it.

Another example is I wrote a book about what my life was like growing up. I mostly wrote it for my kids so when I am gone, they can always read it and learn more about me, their mother.
But once I am gone, I won't be there anymore to answer any questions they might have. So if they ever do read the book, they might have questions, but I won't be here to answer them. It would be nice if my kids took the time to read that book, or any of the ones I have written.

Or when a new book comes out I usually buy everyone that I know a free copy, and it goes on their shelf, no one reads it, and no one calls me to say, oh, the story was cute or I hated it or anything at all. Nothing!!! Not a word. So what Is that about?
I have given many children books as gifts, the parents must read them, right? I always wonder if the child even enjoyed the story and pictures. I have no idea! But, on the other hand, strangers that buy my books will even go to the point of mailing me pictures of their kids reading my books and loving them!

Even though my outlook on this has mostly been with the attitude of, I really don't care, I am happy with what I do, and create. All that really matters is that I enjoy writing my books, doing my crafts and paintings, so that is enough and that it pleases me. But then every once in a while this comes up, well every time I post a new book I got published, and today I just needed to express it. I love writing and I am not going to stop publishing my books.

In the end, we really do care, its nice to hear someone say something nice, right? My mother taught me, that if you are talking to a person, say your at the bank, or whatever and you notice something you like about the person, or what they are wearing, tell them, it will make their day. I make a point to do that. If someone says to you, hey, I like your shirt, or earrings or whatever, you think about that compliment later, right?

To the few that do show support, you know who your are, you are very much appreciated. Thank you. :-)

Simba my Cat

Simba was such a wonderful person cat. :-) The day I had to take him to the vet to put him to sleep was terrible, I did not know what to do, to take him or not to take him. He slept beside me all night, he had not eaten or gone to the bathroom for days, so I took him for that dreadful ride.

I was still worried that I was making a mistake as I was driving, talking to him all the way, as he laid there sleeping.

I took him out of the car and held him in my arms and looked at his beautiful features. All the way he never once looked or changed his expression, even in bed that morning.

I got out of the car and picked him up an held him close,
"we are here Boo", (his nickname) he opens his blue eyes and looks at me and then gave me a big blink and then takes a deep breath and releases it. I knew he was saying it was time and it was ok. So I took him in and held him in my arms, talking to him about everything, and how I loved him, and that he would see his pal, Rusty and brother Skye, and that Lisa would be there looking for him, and during my talking to him, they injected him. His eyes got big when he felt the drug and was gone in a heartbeat. It was so sad but at least he went in peace. I loved him so much. Oh, my dearest Boo, I can hardly stand editing this, as I reread it. I love you so much.

They put him in a beautiful white box to bury him in, and gave me a card with some of his fur. The people there were so kind.

I drove him home and I buried him with flowers.

Lisa Jean
_____

Remembering Lisa Jean and what a wonderful person she was. A great mom and daughter. She had so many accomplishments at such a young age. I am forever proud of her. One of the things she did a short time before the nightclub fire was write a beautiful story about love, friendship and loss. I remember the day she brought it over to me to read, as I read it she stood next to me, and I cried at the end, it was so moving. The nice thing about her too, was she asked her younger sister to illustrate her book. It was an exciting project. I always thought it was meant somehow for her little daughter Zoe Jean. It Is a comforting book that I have shared many times with people who have lost loved ones. I Finally I got it published for her in her memory. If you would like a copy, the title is: Henry and Sara by Lisa Jean Kelly

I also wrote a poem for her:

For Lisa Jean
_____

I Sit
My Face Calm
My Mind Screaming

I See A Girl
Walking Towards Me
Sunglasses
Long Auburn Hair Tied Back

My Heart Leaps
I Stare

I Sit
My Face Cam

My Mind Weeps

I Live
A Smile For The World

My Body Aches
Sadness Leaks Down My Face

Squinting Eyes
To Hold Back The Pain
Of Things I Cannot Erase

Love mom

Grounding

I have been trying the different methods of grounding and will explain how each one felt to me and my results.

This one I would do every morning before I started to work in my office. I would stand in my office and it was very quiet. I did not notice too much sound, and I was feeling well and relaxed. I would close my eyes and stood up straight with my arms own by my side with my palms facing own. I took in a few deep breaths with my nose then exhaled slowly with my nose. I thought about my feet and I could feel them firmly on the floor and they felt warm, my arms felt cool I then spread out my feet wider and bent my knees a little, this made me feel a little off balanced, and it too me a few minutes to feel more stable. I noticed with my eyes open I felt more balanced then I did with them closed. I have noticed this every time I do this exercise that when I bend my knees it makes me feel off balanced. I do not know why, so I would do some of it with my eyes open and then closed. While standing doing this I would have a good feel of my feet and thought about my center and focused my breath to go down to my navel until I found the heaviness there. Once I was able to find that I just stayed like that for about five minutes an shut my eyes and continued to breath in and out. I did not feel my arms as being cool anymore but all of a sudden I could hear the ticking of the clock in my office as very loud. It became the only sound I heard. This I think brought me right into the present moment listening to the clock ticking. I then open my eyes and I felt very relaxed. To me this felt like a very successful practice of grounding.

In the afternoon after lunch I would practice laying on my bed with my arms at my sides with my eyes closed. I am trying to ground myself by feeling my center and also visualizing roots going from my body deep into the ground and reaching the core of the earth to feel the warmth and to draw the energy back into myself and also breathing out to release negative energy out into the air. This visualization I found hard to do at first, and I can visualize most things. I have a great imagination and can see just about anything I think of but doing the roots was harder. So after much practice of laying on my bed and breathing in and out, I was able to locate my center each time and I would think about my roots going deep and how I found it to work for me was to think of my energy going down deep into the earth with each breath and then coming up into me from the earth with my breathing out. This I could feel, and the position I found best was laying on my back with my arms an my sides and palms down and my knees bent. I noticed the sounds in my house but only in the background, and then they faded out the more I relaxed and was able to picture the energy going down and coming back into me as good new energy and releasing the old energy. I found this method very relaxing and I feel I will be better able to visualize the roots the more I do this. I also practice this before bed which makes me feel ready to go to sleep.

I am finding the more I do grounding the more solid I feel. In the sense that I also would picture my center and the center of the universe and pictured it like the sun and all the outside things around me were the planets and stars. It was almost easy to picture it as a pinwheel, where the center was the middle of the pinwheel and if you twirled my body around my arms and legs would be going around my center in a circle. So if I visualized the pinwheel or sun as the center I then found that by feeling more solid, I could concentrate more on my energy a roots going into the earth. After a few second of doing this I noticed when my eyes are closed I see purple in my vision, it is like purple clouds. This purple stayed with me through the whole time I was doing it. By trying different visualizations like the pinwheel and the sun I think I was able to do a good grounding.

I liked the grounding practice of looking at trees and to imagine their roots. This was a interesting grounding for me. It is cold here so I stood at my patio door and looked out into the backyard which is full of trees. The day was not sunny, and I had just done the grounding on my bed and that went well so I decided to try this. Each time I do this one, I get the same results. So I stood at the door, shut my eyes and stood with my feet apart and my hands down by my sides. I was not cold but felt comfortable. The TV was playing in the background which I did not notice after a few minutes. As I breathed in and out with my eyes shut I bent my knees a little. I felt pretty steady on my feet. Once I located the center I opened my eyes and looked at the trees. I know that as big as a tree is, that is how big the roots are under the ground. I pictured the roots from each tree and how big they are for each tree. The ground must be a massive system of roots It is amazing to picture it. Then I shut my eyes and pictured the roots but I did not see the roots but orange and yellow and the only way I can explain it is what like I was traveling through this maze of color that was moving by me. Like in the movies when you see the space ship do a time warp and the stars just fly by in a streak. This was not a streak but solid orange and yellow like small dots and I would move forward through it at a fast speed. I felt like I was traveling down into the earth. I felt unbalanced and touched the door to stay myself. It was not sunny at all outside, the day was overcast so I cannot say that I was seeing the sun through my eyelids. I opened my eyes and shut them again and I could do it all over again. I do not know what I was seeing or why, and I think this was very interesting so I will be practicing this one again to note my results in my journal.

Essay: Shielding

I have used shielding in the past but not very much now. I am glad to be doing a class and learning how to use it in a conscious manner. Years ago, when confronted with negative energies I dealt with it by laughing it off, or ignoring it, or walking away.

The most negative energy I felt was when I was apartment shopping. I had checked out this place and it was great, big rooms, a large yard with a garden. Perfect, or so I thought. So I brought my husband over to see it, and we were just about to sign the lease, and all of a sudden the most evil feeling came over me. It is hard to explain except that it was dark and scary and I just said to my husband, no, I don't want it.

Just like that, we left. Nothing was ever said about it, he never asked why. Which is strange in itself, but I have told many people this story. I did not know anything at that time about having a protective shield.

So I have been practicing doing a shield. I am finding it very easy to ground myself now. At first it was difficult to picture roots going down into the earth from my feet or hands etc. I don't know why, but now I can think of them and I can see them going right to the center of the earth. Presto!

So I do that first and its pretty amazing to see that in my mind, and then I have been working on picturing a oblong bubble around my body. I can be standing up or laying down. It does not matter to me. Then as I picture it, I imagine the bubbles around me, it looks like a bubble that you used to blow as a kid from a container of liquid soap. So it has the iridescent color and I picture something

coming at it like a stone but its negative energy and when the stone hits it, the bubble indents a little and the the stone bounces right off. As I am inside the this bubble it is funny to see the negative energy bouncing off of it going off into all directions.
So I practice this and making believe that things come at me.

Now to come to the real test. There are not many people who I can test this on now because of the Covid-19. But I do have my husband. :-) We get along great, so the only time I figured I could practice on him is when he is watching his hockey games.
He loves to share the games with me as he watches it, and I am not really that interested in it, but I like to keep him company so I will play a game on my phone.
So he will say, at a certain plays of the game, look at that! A fight, did you see it? What that guy did? And I know he is not expecting me to jump up and look so it's the perfect time to try out the shield. So I shut my eyes and did the bubble and pictured the words just bouncing off of me. It was like I was there, but I did not have to be a part of what was going on. I could now focus on my game not not get as distracted. This works great anytime you go out, if you get anxiety shopping or in whatever situation, you should learn how to shield.

Sometimes when people get into a conversation about anything it is sometimes hard to join into the conversation. I can get impatient waiting and now if I do the shielding it does not bother me if I don't get my say. I don't know why, it works like that but it seems that the going back and forth of the conversation, the excitement of it does not matter so much to me anymore. To me the shielding is protecting me from getting myself in a negative mood and agitated with someone else.

When I do the shielding I do it this way. I picture the roots first, breathing and relaxing. Once I feel calm I pictures the bubble going around my whole body. I don't feel either warm or cold, just comfortable. Because its a bubble and iridescent the colors make me feel happy. I can see the colors swirling around and just focusing on that distracts me from anything else going on around me. By getting into this bubble its like I just leave the room. It becomes very peaceful and puts a little smile on my face.
To me its more quiet, I do not hear any sound or vibrations as of yet in this practice. So if the bubble is around me and I push my arms out and palms up I can stretch the bubble out and push in and out on it and it goes in and out with my pressure. If you could see me walking with it around me I would look like a walking bubble going into a store. When I stop to think about the bubble it disappears, but I can bring it back in a flash. Now I do a dragon shield, using a dragon image around me, feels more like myself then using the bubble.

Stories of Becoming Aware

Today I cuddled with my cat, Simba (Boo). As I laid in my bed waking up, my cat Simba came up and wanted to go under the covers as usual. So I lifted up the blankets and he proceeded to go right under and then turned around and laid across my arm that was stretched out, as I was laying on my right side.

So, today I thought I will just relax and enjoy the beauty of my cat.

I started to really look at him and see how majestic he really is. As I petted him and rubbed his neck and back, he looked so peaceful and at times he would look at me straight in the eyes and just stare back at me. If I blinked he would blink. It was like he was saying everything is fine.

I feel so blessed to be able to be in that warm space with such a wonderful animal who has so much trust to be beside me, who in comparison to him I must seem like a giant. As I lay there looking at him in wonder and awe at his perfection and beauty nothing else matters for these moments in the outside world.

I think if only I could be so perfect, he is just amazing to look at with such carved out features like he was made from marble. His wide nose, long lashes, and him in my arms and then he rewards me with a soothing purr. What a honor to have this cat as part of my family. He falls asleep and I lay listening to his breathing, in and out. If I shut my eyes you would think he was a person, he sounds just like a person breathing. I lay my hand gently on his back and he does not wake, a beautiful moment of sharing with him has increased my appreciation of his life and that of all animals.

It is raining out today, so I have gone outside to sit in our screened in porch. I shut my eyes an breath in the fresh scent of the air, its cool as I feel it go in though my nose and down the back of my throat. I can hear all the birds singing and chirping their spring calls. Its so peaceful and quiet except for the dripping of the rain hitting the roof of this room and also the sound of the rain hitting the surface of the water in our fish pond.

It is very calm and the air is still as I look around. I notice the moss growing on my Star Circle, which is a huge circle I made with blocks on the ground and the edges form 12 points, it looks like a large star. The rain is giving everything a darker brighter color and it is beautiful to see. The tree branches are so dark in contrast with the sky behind them and I can see the tiny sprouts of new leaf buds growing on them. They should come out in a few weeks time. As I listen I thank the rain for bringing water to the plants and trees and for the creatures of the earth, and for cleaning the air and ground and for giving me this chance to appreciate these moments to step outside of my busy life.

Today I have gone out and fed the birds. I have filled the feeder and put out new suets and filled the sunflower containers. As soon as I walked away Chickadees were at the feeder grabbing the sunflower seeds. So I chose to sit on the lawn for a time and see what goes on. About ten minutes later I see a Titmouse in the cherry tree and soon enough he lands on the suet. I cannot hear any other sound of spring yet. It will be exciting when the spring peepers start up. There are no insects are flying around yet, it must be too cold. The squirrels are in the trees next door and I am sure they will come over here and pick up the seeds that fall from the feeder. I am waiting to see if our little chipmunk comes out from under the deck. The chipmunk lives under the deck and our cat, Blueberry loves to sit and look for him. One time last year she caught him, and

I had to run out and save him. As soon as I yelled out to Blueberry to drop him, she did and he ran as fast as he could back under the deck. Pretty soon Morning Doves flew and sat high up in the tree branches. I think they are waiting for me to leave. I know as soon as I go inside they will be on the feeder. I love hearing the cooing sounds they make. Then way up high I can hear the sharp sounds of a bird, and I strain to see what it could be. I don't know what birds make that sound. Finally after some time I see a pair of Cardinals. So now I know their call. To me having birds around remind me of what beauty they bring to us with their colors and songs. We are so lucky to be able to have them come close enough so we can enjoy seeing them. They are so brave to live and survive the elements especially in the winter. I alway make sure they have food all winter long. My mother was a bird watcher and she taught me all the bird names and how to feed them. I also wrote a book about building a squirrel proof bird feeder that really works and is also kind to squirrels because they get to eat all the seeds that fall of the feeder without eating all your birdseed.

The weather has been warming up and we had a really warm winter. Any snow that we got melted right away. It actually seemed like fall all winter. So today is pretty nice out and I thought I would move all my houseplants that can be outside for the summer. Plus repotting ones that need bigger pots.
I have grown two citrus trees from seed. The are both now about four feet tall and I am hoping they will flower and produce some fruit. I do not know what kind of citrus trees I grew, and should have written it down what kind of seeds I planted. They needed to

be repotted, so I bought potting soil and got two bigger pots and removed the trees from the old pots. I noticed how much the roots have grown since I last repotted them. It is amazing to see them all curled around so tightly in a ball, they hardly have any soil left. As I put in the new soil and replanted and watered them and set them out in the sun, I noticed how shiny and bright the leaves are. They have a lot of new growth on the top and they must know its springtime. I will enjoy watching them grow this year and hope they flower later on. It is exciting to save your citrus seeds and see if they will grow. Last year I got a avocado seed to grow. I just put them in a pot with soil and one grew. It was doing so well, and then all the leaves fell off. I thought I was not giving it enough water, so I looked it up. Actually its not suppose to get much water and I was killing it. So all winter it sat in my house with no leaves looking dead But now I see it is getting a little green growth where the leaves were before. Now I know water it good and then let it dry out completely. It does not like water.

I am also regrowing some vegetables. You can buy chives and cut off the ends and put them in water to grow, and soon you will have chives to use again. I am also doing this with celery. It is amazing and fun to work with plants and getting rewarded with fruits, vegetables and flowers.

Since its a nice day, I thought I would go out into my flower garden and see what survived the winter. I started a new garden last year, wanting to make a new larger area to grow more plants. As I walk around I am noticing new growth on the blueberry bushes. They are forming tiny little leaves already. So it is the same as the other early spring trees that are budding now. I am excited to see the

Pussy Willow tree I planted has a few catkins on it, they are my favorite. The catkins are like little soft cat toes. The use to grow in the woods when I was a kid. There is also a little plant that grows that has the same type of flowers on them. I called them cat toes. I have no idea what they are, only they grow wild and are very small, like a clover plant. My new Iris look good and also the lilies are up. My Bee Balm has grown bigger already and I see the Rhubarb plant looks great. I need to get more of those. I never had them grow well for me, but this one looks like its doing well. There is nothing like a homemade rhubarb pie. My project the last few years was digging up Milkweed to grow to help the Monarch butterflies. I finally got them to come back up and now I have quite a few. I have some in this garden but they have not come up. They seem to come up later then the other spring plants.

One of my favorites is Chicory. It grows near the roads and is very hard to dig up. It is usually in the hardest soil. I love the blue color of its flowers. Last year my husband and I were up in Maine and we got lost on this dirt road, and when we were turning the car around there was some chicory growing in soft soil! I said stop the car and got out and got one plant and wrapped it in a plastic bag and gave it water. When we got home I planted it, and to my surprise it came up and is growing. That probably made me the happiest to see today. I love being out in the garden enjoying the flowers and plants. It is the renewal of life after a long winter of being inside. Spring fever is the best feeling to have.

Its time to start the vegetable seeds inside to plant in May. I have gathered the pots and containers and seeds an I am ready to get my hands in the soil.

I love seeing all the little seeds. When I was young I use to help my parents plant the garden. I loved planting all the seeds and learned to recognize most of them. Beet seeds are all bumpy and carrots seeds sleek and small. The black and white bean seeds, but some are all brown or reddish and some pure white, depending on the kind. I love seeds.

I am starting this year sweet peppers, cumin and melon seeds. I need to pick up some other kinds but this I will start today.

It is so enjoyable to be in the sun on my porch and playing in the dirt! It will be exciting to see them when they first pop up and to care and water them. They are like babies taking so much care and love. This is another way to appreciate the life around us by seeing a plant grow from a little seed to a mature plant.

On another note, I was able to buy from our local seed shop this corn seed. It is called Montana Cudo Corn. I bought it because it is descended from a historic Native American variety. It has blue spotted kernels and some of them look just like a eagle on the kernels. That is why it is considered scared to the Native Americans.

Today I am going to check out the woods in my front yard. Years ago we use to have a lawn, but I said, as I get older I am not planning on mowing the lawn. So I let it go wild and I planted trees. Now it is beautiful woods. I made a path in the middle that goes around a bed of flowers, that are mostly lilies and plants that come up every year. The outer areas are covered with Periwinkle. The Periwinkle I brought here to my home from my parents house. My dad brought it home one day from a construction site he was working on and planted it near our street. It is so nice to have a plant that came from my dad.

But every spring I have to cut out the little bushes that seem to grow overnight so it does not get too wild. I have a bench I can sit on and see the traffic out on the main road, but right here it is peaceful and is like being in another world. As I sit I see the trees starting to bud, the pines are still green of course, and the Dogwood is showing signs of life again.

The lilies are growing down by the street and the bushes in front block the view of my home from the street. The front is lined with Rose of Sharon. I planted them when they were about 10 inches high and now they are around 15 feet tall.

My front yard is now my own little piece of the wild woods. I have seen possums and skunks out in these woods. The other day we actually had for the first time wild turkeys come into our yard. It was amazing, they are so beautiful and huge. It is late afternoon and the sun is going across the west and will set in a few hours. If I go out there when the sun sets, on some days the sky is a beautiful blue and pink. Along the sidewalk the Hosta plants are just poking up and they get so big an have those long purple flowers on them.

We get lots of Humming birds in the summertime. It is nice to have woods as we can see different types of life such as the time we had a Coyote sitting out front and then another time we had a Fisher Cat up in our tree, and many of rabbits. Now that I am sitting here for a time I have noticed the lone tulip that has bloomed with red and white petals. Also the bamboo has grown quite a bit. It is good to take time to just sit and look around, it gives me a chance to appreciate the beauty that is all around me even in my front yard. Nature is wonderful and its just there waiting for us to appreciate it.

Essay: Honoring the Seasons

I am looking for spring as soon as the month of March arrives. I can't wait for spring. It is the best time of year when everything starts over.

The first thing I noticed is that the sun is shining in the sky longer and longer each day. The sun's rays also feel warmer on my skin. Some days for us in March are warm and some days rainy and cold with or without wind.

Soon enough, the first signs of life I see are my Daffodils coming up and also the early spring flowers such as Crocus. Some of the Dandelions are turning green. I have even seen a Dandelion bloom in January, which is crazy for our northern climate.

Then in April the real signs of spring is when I first hear the peepers. That is the best sound to hear, it makes me know spring is here for sure.

Then the next sign we get are the Robins coming back from the south. All of a sudden they will be hopping over the ground looking for worms.

I also look for signs of spring by looking at the trees. I first will notice them getting buds which make them look fatter. Soon enough baby leaves will sprout. In myself, spring fever sets in, and I want to plant and start my seeds and can't wait to plan out the garden. Its funny, these desires of doing spring chores do not happen till spring. I have no desire to go clean the yard in January, its not till it seems the weather changes and the days get longer that spring fever happens.

I wonder if it has something to do with the longer days of light. We are probably affected with spring just as the new plants and animals.

I love spring as it makes me feel full of energy. I love cleaning the yard and making plans for the flower and vegetable gardens. I also love getting new baby chicks in the spring. Its always fun to enjoy baby chicks, they are so adorable.

Springtime and the change of weather always gives me more energy and makes me want to do more things and this includes any magickal practices I like to do. Its a great time to sage your home to clear out old energies from the winter.

My Green Altar

Setting up my green altar has been very interesting. I like the idea of having it as it will give me a place to mediate an set my intentions for the day and work outside. It also gives me the time to reflect and appreciate the life around me. Life seem so busy, that I do not always take the time out to focus and enjoy it. So this is a very positive project to do is to set up my green altar.

It will also give me a place to set out my crystals when there is a full moon for them to gather moonlight and get recharged.

I am going to plan out how I want it to be. I would like the altar to be as natural as possible since it is going to be outdoors. I am going to use a old garden chair I have so I can sit and meditate when I light candles or burn sage. I am going to use a Abalone shell to burn the sage on, it was a gift from a good friend, Cady and now I can put it to good use. I am also going to use a pagoda I have to light a candle, I am happy to use this as it was my daughters. I am also going to use a picture of my beloved cat, Skye and some of my favorite rocks. I feel that my altar is reflecting myself. This is going to be fun to set up and use.

Now the it is set up, I like to mediate first and I start out by lighting a candle and I burn some sage. When I do these things I look at the picture of my cat and remember him and tell him I love him. Then I light the candle in my daughters pagoda, I think of her too and tell her my thought are with her and I love her, then I will sit and meditate. I start smelling the sage and I listen to the sounds of nature. This I try to enjoy and disregard The other sounds that are not part of my natural surroundings.

Dragon Eyes

I like to do different crafts like painted stained glass, hand building using clay and sea scapes using rocks and drift wood. I found a new creative project that has sparked my interest and its painted rocks. I see them left around places like stores, parks and the post office out on the ground. Its like a faze going around in Rhode Island by a group called rock hounds or something like that. They leave a painted rock and your suppose to take it and post it on facebook, of where you found it and then you can leave it somewhere else. So I thought I would try doing painted rocks

I went onto You Tube and found some people showing you how they paint rocks. One lady does dragon eyes and that is the one I want to learn how to do. Another person does dragon eyes but uses clear glass gems instead of rocks.

I am going to try both methods.

On the first one you just need to find a round stone or whatever shape you want it to be. Then you paint a white circle on it, and add details and colors you would like to use. It is rather easy to do. You can use regular acrylic paints but I like the painted pens.

You really need to follow a video to see how to actually do it so it comes out awesome.

With the gem method you use nail polish. First I got some clear glass gems, they sell them in all the craft stores.

On the back of the gem you paint a black line for the pupil of the dragons eye and then around the edges you make jagged streaks with different colors. Once it is dry you paint over that with black nail polish. When it is dry you can turn it over and you have a glass dragons eye.

I liked the rock version of the dragons eye the best. I think they are more colorful and look like a real dragons eye much better then the gems.

Religion

On religion, I was raised Methodist, can't help but believe what we are taught as kids, like Santa Claus and the tooth fairy till the day your dad tells you they are not real. that was terrible!!!

Anyhow going to church as a teenager I was more disappointed with the people then the church. I remember the guy down the street was one of the pastors. He stopped on the street one day when I was out walking and I was happy to see him, and in my mind I thought he missed me at church, as I never hardly went, but you know started bitching at me that if I did not go and tithe they were going to take me off the list.

I was so mad I told my mom that I was never going to church again, and I never did.

Years later I joined the Jehovah witnesses, that lasted for like 4 years, till I got kicked out, the people were nice but I could not believe that if you were not of their religion, you were all bound for hell.

Plus when I was getting divorced, I had a boyfriend and that did not go over well, the men or head guys came to visit me, to try to get me back, before they kicked me out, I could not understand how it was wrong to care for someone, and have it be wrong, so even though I was not technically divorced yet, but separated, and having a guy on the side was not allowed, so that did not set right with them. So I said, "whatever," and they kicked me out. That means anyone that was your friend there, was not able to associate with me anymore. Like I gave a fuck, if they did not or not. Anyhow my life went on just fine.

So I believe in God or whoever is out there, and I believe my daughter who I lost at the age of 27 in the nightclub station fire in 2003 is still with us in spirit. So there has to be something there. I feel her presence and others around me at times, even pets. So something is going on in the afterlife.

For myself, I do not go to any churches, do not like their attitudes at all, I have found most times if a person is a ass and judgmental they are a christian. Most people who give you shit or judge you or criticize others are so called christians.

All those people out there in politics who are condemning everyone say they are christians but in reality are so far from it.

One thing I did learn was in scripture and that I believe is: Love covers all, all the prophecies were fulfilled and love is the # one rule and that it is not for us to judge others, ever!!! God will do the judging.

We need to show compassion.

I might not like what some people do, but its not up to me to judge them, I don't have to hang out with people that are jerks but still that is their journey not mine.

So in the end, I do have some christian beliefs, I live my life by what I feel is the right thing to do, and what feels right in my heart.

I practice Native American traditions, and also some Wizardly thoughts and whatever I believe in which is tons of stuff. As John Lennon said, "

"I believe in everything until it's disproved. So I believe in fairies, the myths, dragons. It all exists, even if it's in your mind. Who's to say that dreams and nightmares aren't as real as the here and now?" — John Lennon

I really like the books, The Four Agreements by Don Miguel Ruiz" and Ask And It Is Given by Ester and Jerry Hicks." I recommend these two book as very important to read.

Some of the books I wrote like The Kings Journey, was told to me in a semi-sleep by my cat who passed. So I am open to that.

Then once I went to a class at a local sort of nature store, by a woman who teaches communication with animals etc,

as I was sitting there with like 80 people she said to me, (I was like shocked). "I do not know why you are even here, I am so happy you are but you are so powerful and I honored to have you at my class", and she said something like that 3 times, it was sort of embarrassing, so I guess I might be a powerful wizard after all! :-)

Anyhow I go by my heart in my beliefs rather then any of men's teachings.

I also believe in Aliens, I use to belong to Mufon, and I have passed their exam to go out and investigate sightings, but have not done that for a long time. Life got busy.

Also was vegetarian as I really believe we should not harm animals but am not a very good one. I wrote a cookbook for the animals on how to become a vegetarian and all about the treatment of animals in factory farming. I do my best on that end, its a constant struggle but most days are meatless.

Inmates

I as I said before I run a business for inmates and these are a few replies I got back that I liked.

A new saying I just learned from one of my dragons (Charles Street) OMFD!
(oh my fucking dragons!) love it! :-)

A cool poem shared to me recently by Ed Bryant.
"Books take you to distant lands. Right at the tip of your hands.
They teach you about different places discover new cultures other races.
Take a journey open the cover, let you mind wander through the portals of time. One never knows what they might find. Venture to Islands, rivers, lakes and oceans. Or let the prose tangle your emotions. Reading can be one of life's pleasures and may lead to unexpected treasures."

:-)

"I wish I had a Dragon in my life a lot sooner." (To me (Stardragon) from James D. Walker)

James Walker is on a show on Netflix, the show is called: I am a Killer/Blackout.
He wrote this to me;
There was a time in my life when this would have never happened, but if it had not been for you ordering a book for me. It helped me change into the person I am now. So let me put it like this: There once was a beautiful dragon and she was a Stardragon who believed in the good in everyone. Most dragons have a fire that burns but Stardragon's fire burned with hope and motivation. Once touch by this fire you are forever changed and encourage that you have the strength to do anything.
Thank you, Thank you for your services and loyalty.
James Walker

From Dustin, on a more personal note, its nice to see a fellow pagan (norse pagan here) doing business for inmates. Your letter has such a strong energy, its like bubblegum and vodka had a love child! Thank you for all you do, may the universe never fail to mystify you.

Some Wizardly quotes that I like:

Destiny is not a matter of chance, it is a matter of choice; it is not a thing to be waited for, it is a thing to be achieved, - William Jennings Bryant

Draco Dormiens Nunquam Titillandu!
(never tickle a sleeping dragon)
And young dragons don't understand, if humans don't want to be eaten, why are they made of meat and treasure? (wizards of the coast)

"Why you should not tickle a sleeping dragon- Sleeping dragons when tickled, open one eye, and if they think you might be tasty, your gone in a flash! And then they smile! And if they don't think your tasty they will crunch you up in one bite, and then spit you out, and then they will laugh! And go back to sleep" (stardragon)

Magical spell for protection against unwanted opinions:
Take a deep cleansing breath, then say the words: "Did I fucking ask you? Repeat until desired effect is achieved".
Blessed Be.

Remember a letter is never early, or late. It arrives precisely when it means to.
Meddle not in the affairs of Dragons, for you are crunchy and taste good with ketchup.

Step over ants, put worms back in the grass, rescue baby caterpillars, release spiders back into your garden, open windows or bees to fly home. They are all little souls that deserve a life too. :-)

Journals

It is good to keep a journal of our thoughts, emotions and dreams. In parts of this book, I will write out some of my journals, just things I was thinking about and also my dreams.

Journal Entries throughout 2007/2009

Oct 4

Beautiful summer day. Today I found out I was accepted into the Grey School of Wizardry!
I am very excited. The classes all look very interesting. It looks like I will learn so many things. I cannot wait to start.

How did I learn of the school? Well, my granddaughters grandmother is Wiccan and we went to a craft show. We brought home a flyer with the school's information on it. So I checked it out on the website and I loved it. So I signed up and picked the name of Stardragon.

Oct 5

Today I got my granddaughter for the weekend and we are going to my sisters for a lobster dinner.
Dinner was excellent, my granddaughter went down to the pond and got soaking wet, the pond was so much fun.

Then we are going with my daughter to see the Lippizaner Stallions. I am taking Mimulus for the ride! Only one more section and I will have finished level one in my Bach Flower Essence classes I am sure Lisa would be proud.

The horse show was excellent, but my granddaughter seemed bored, so I was a little disappointed. It's something to see, the horses work so hard and the riders are all fired up, well at least we saw it.

The Mimulas worked wonders. I have to admit it works, a relaxing ride, I was not nervous at all.

Oct 6

We were up late, so of course I was tired today.

Joe and Destiny were over and I cooked breakfast. Joe Sr. was over and Joe fixed his car and Joe took Zoe Jean to the bike shop.

I mailed out my book order, went to the library, Job Lot and got some nice journals.

I got the Bach Flower essences copied into my computer folder. Now I can print out the essences that I make for someone.

Took Zoe Jean to riding lessons and Bob's for some more clothes.

Came home and made dinner.

Greg has a gig tonight.

Lots of reading to do between my first class of wizardry and the last section of the Bach remedies.

Oct 7

Today Zoe Jean woke me up, that is a change, she usually sleeps late.

She was excited as our baby chickens are hatching, So we went out to see them on the porch, five hatched so far this morning. Its awesome as we watched them peck through the shells. Zoe Jean fed Tigerlily our pony and gave the chickens some grain.

Last night she was crying, upset about her dad. She says he has to go to court on the 15th for a old DUI cause he never completed his classes. She is worried he will go to jail. I tried to ease her worries. If it happens I told her to tell him to let her stay with me and I will drive her to school until he gets out. I know she doesn't not want to stay with his wife.

This morning Zoe Jean and I went to Mr. B's for breakfast. She had her favorite, egg, cheese and bacon on a French toast bagel. I ended up having a butter spinach bagel and a coffee.

We went home and Jackie stopped by, so we went to Walmart with her. She got Zoe Jean some nice boots and clothes. I got some stuff too. On the way there Jackie was talking about when she was in school and how she would notice that whatever the weather was, it would somehow effect how the kids acted. Isn't it weird she said that as I have to write what the weather is everyday in my Journal for the Wizardry School. Then we went to D'Angelso too and got subs.

Greg is going to take Zoe Jean roller blading. I am staying home to relax, and read, etc.

The day is still cloudy, and overcast. Zoe Jean caught the white chicken, we cut her wings as she was flying over the six foot fence. So much to write about, it would take forever.

I am going to try to finish my lessons on Bach. Level one will be done. :-)

Jackie said the flower remedy I made for her for sleeping really worked fine. Also the ones that helped her feel better that I gave her the other day. So all good reports on people using the remedies.

Destiny called, she cleaned her apartment and has bags of clothes for Zoe Jean to check out.

Zoe Jean and Greg cut out their Halloween pumpkins. Greg bought her a 50 pound pumpkin today. Its huge.

Zoe Jean is making a elastic shooter and we went to the store to get clothespins for it.

Feels so good to be doing this journal, doing the Bach classes and studying wizardry. Kids can do the classes too but I don't know how they would be able to do them, the classes have so much involved, its like college. I thinks its great they offer them to kids but It seems too difficult. I wonder how the higher levels are going to be. The first essay will be on my journal. I hope I know how to write a essay. I bought another journal just for dreams.

Doesn't seem like I dream much, still doing the vegetarian diet. Its easy now like in one month.

Oct 8

Cloudy, today, cool but not cold. I slept well, no dreams at all the last few days, waiting to write in my dream journal. But I need to add a dream I had a few weeks ago about flying. It was awesome! Slept till 8:30, Zoe Jean was already up, so I made breakfast. I found my calligraphy book so I got a journal to practice in. I played some piano. I am feeling really great and happy about all of this. It makes me feel good. I looked at the 2007 spring edition of the Grey School newspaper, and printed it out to read later. Its very interesting, I wish they had paper copies of it. I might be able to get a school ring.

I am such a kid!!!

It seems like all these things I am going to do, I have been doing all my life and wanted to do. Its been in my heart now maybe I have a way to bring it all together.

Zoe Jean goes home today, :-(but we had a great weekend. Next weekend she is staying home to camp out with her Dad.

Then Greg is taking us all, with Trevor to to Seattle.

Zoe Jean's dad told his wife, she was with the other grandmother as she thinks she spends too much time with me. Well her day will come. She is such a "B". Lisa would be so mad that, he does not put his foot down. But he is doing better as now Zoe Jean has her phone.

Jackie went to PA. for a few days to see her son.

So at 5 pm I took Zoe Jean home, and she brought her 50 pound pumpkin with her. Her dad was there and seemed quiet, her stepmother was there painting pumpkins and unfriendly as normal. I helped Zoe Jean set up her new desk lamp and picked up her room. I saw Joey and Destiny on the way home.

Greg and I went to the cemetery near the Legion Hall, to look for the "shadow person". And I taped recorded but got nothing or did not see anything either, but did see a nice black and white cat.

Came home and watched the movie "Ghost Ship".

Oct 9

It looks like it rained last night, sun is out now. Its cool and it looks like a nice day coming.

I woke Zoe Jean up this morning, I called her for 15 minutes but she got up and caught the bus. (no one ever wakes her up for school)

I finished copying pages from the Grey School newspaper and put it into a folder. Now that is done, lots of great articles to read. So much to learn.

Busy day, errands, paint, books etc. Time for a shower.

Oct 10

Rainy day, it must have rained lots last night, everything is wet. Birds are singing, cats are playing. Lisa's birthday is today. Life seems so unfair. Lisa's gone, why? why? why? I miss Lisa Jean, she is my hero.

Woke Zoe Jean up at 7, she was already up. Talked to Destiny, she remembered Lisa's birthday. :-) Zoe Jean wants me to come visit today. Her dad said to come at 5:00, I know why so late, Mel will be at work :-)

Cady emailed me last night to chat. I love that girl. I wish she lived closer. I want to go see her.

Got to do my first essay on wizards. I am nervous, I want to do a good job. Not sure how. Destiny says to do at least three paragraphs, Well, I have to the feed the animals, do books. My friend June is coming over to watch "Pretty Woman".

I put yellow roses and a balloon and lit a candle on Lisa's grave. What a way to spend her birthday. I remember the day she was born, she was so little, and had such a little nose, I called her my little button nose.

Went to Destinys, then to see Zoe Jean.

Her dad was there, we had a cake for Lisa. He sang happy birthday. On the way home we had a talk about how the stepmother does not like me going there, well it all came out. I will not ever not got see Zoe Jean. Her dad says I can go there whenever I want.

I am home now, glad to relax.
I will see Joey tomorrow with Jackie.

Oct 11
Got up early, rainy, wet, damp. Jackie and I went to Joe's for lunch, we had Chinese. I brought brownies. Did my first essay this morning, got a 100. I am so happy. Lisa would be proud.
Zoe Jean is home from school. I also wrote a lot on my online journal today.

Magickal name.
I name myself Stardragon!
I have said it now on once
Stardragon! shall I be.
I have now said it twice.
I am Stardragon! I have said it now thrice.
And what I say three times is true!
By all the powers of land and sea.
As I do will, so mote it be!

Oct 12
No rain, damp and cool this morning.
Well today went well, June and I watched a movie, gregs gig was cancelled, so we stayed in, watched a movie, "Next with Nicholas Cage. Zoe Jean has her friend sleeping over and her dad was setting up a fire. He said I was right about it all and I can go see Zoe Jean anytime I want. Tomorrow Zoe Jean and her dad are camping out at some friends house. Next week I have her for the

whole week. I am tired, a busy day, stressful with the situation with the dad and stepmother. I worry about Zoe Jean and I am taking some remedies. I wrote my essay on choosing my magickal name.

Oct 14

Nice sunny day but cold. Greg and I had a great day yesterday, went to the mall, greg got a shirt, I got some sage and incense. We had lunch, awesome tofu at the mall's cafeteria. I saw Jerry Verdi there, she was nice. Then we went to Exeter Rhode Island to find Mercy Brown's grave. We found it! Then came home and had supper. So today was relaxing, Zoe Jean had fun camping. I also got my mystical alter set up. I just need a few more things. I cleaned all the bureaus in my room and Lisa's little table looks nice. Next Sunday we will be in Seattle. It should be a blast. Can't wait to see the mountains.

Oct 15

Nice day, sunny and cool.
Got up early and took Zoe Jean to school, 2 hours late there was a accident on the bridge. The day flew by, pick up Zoe Jean, did piano lessons. Got her play station 2 and the sing along dance pad. She loves it. They found two bullets at Zoe Jean's school in the vending machine. That is weird.

Oct 21

We are in Seattle Washington! A beautiful day, and a long flight! Six hours from New Jersey to here. They gave us a Mustang GT, silver black metallic for a rental. It was funny, we were standing at the counter going to rent a car and Zoe Jean says lets get a sports car, and that is what they gave us.

The hotel pool is broken, that sucks as I picked this hotel for its pool. Tomorrow we are going to Mt. Rainer, if its nice out, I can't wait to see it. Also Mt. Saint Helens, the Space Needle, etc. Hope its a fun week. Trevor and Zoe Jean are having fun. She is a little annoying, and is making me mad, I think she is just tired. Talked to Zoe Jean's grandmother, she said her dad was working at her house and that him and his wife are not speaking, and that Zoe Jean might be with me more this coming week.

Driving Zoe Jean back and forth each day to school is a hassle but I don't care, I love having her around and she likes it too. The round trip to school and back is fifty miles. But worth every minuet of it. I took a relaxing bath, I am so tired. In the mail on Saturday my dragons knife came it, its so cool and also the crystal wand. Awesome! I am going to miss my cats this week.

Joey fixed the gate post, no other news.

Oct 24

Seattle, Washington! Cloudy, still dark, just getting light out, looks like another nice day. Yesterday we went to Mt. Saint Helens. Its so awesome and wonderful. I never thought I would be here and see these mountains. We walked some trails and got as close as possible to the crater. The mountain was erupting they say, we could see steam coming out of the dome.

We went to some gift shops and got everyone a gift. I spent a lot! Zoe Jean and Trevor love all the little interesting things they have. In Seattle she bought a nice journal and she is writing poetry! She really writes well. Everyone at home is fine, Charlie, Destiny's dog is sick, he went to the vets and now seems better. Destiny loves that dog so much! Zoe Jean's dad is at his mothers again this week. I wonder what is going to happen with this situation. Zoe Jean goes home on Sunday and back to school. If he works away again I hope he lets her stay with me. Jackie will be leaving for Florida in a few weeks. That will stink, she is gone a long time.

Nov 6
Rainy day, cool.
I have not written in this as much I have been doing a online journal. Zoe Jean is still with me, her dad leaves for Nebraska for work for a week. I love having her around. Book sales are way down, cannot figure out why. Jackie came over to watch a movie today.

Nov 7
Busy day again, got to settle in and do my next essay. Greg told me he was proud of me, not eating meat! Isn't that weird, its nice to hear. :-)

Dec 14
Snowing. I finally got time to get here and write, I am better on keeping up with my on-line journal.
I am studying to do three essays for my classes. I bought a bamboo chair, for my room, cleaned the top of my desk and put my candles and dragons, shells, a incense burner that Cady got me and I put a clay lizard I made over the lamp. Enjoying myself greatly, got to do this more. One essay will be on the philosophers stone, one on Sir Isaac Newton and the other one a a shield volcano. So Awesome! Today I am going to look for a Citrine stone for a study spell. Will take Zoe Jean to Seven Arrows for tea.

March 21 2008

I have been very neglectful keeping this journal as you can see from the dates. Also my on-line journal, but I do that one more often. It was Zoe Jean's birthday yesterday. Zoe Jean's dad and grandmother came over for dinner and he slept over, It's nice having peace in the family. I wish Lisa was here too enjoy it. Spring is coming I have some raking to do but its very windy and cold today. Good Friday today, no school so nice to relax!

One of the odd things that has happened. When I wrote out my information on a index card for PayPal (did it put it away) then when I looked at it later, I said, who wrote this? It was not my handwriting at all. So weird. I wonder it is is Lisa's. It could be hers. I feel Lisa around so much, but I think when I feel her, its like I feel a solid being of her. I can picture her but I feel this solidness. And I feel really sad at the same time. At first I did not know why, but now I think its her being "here." You know it just comes over me. I organized my books yesterday in the spare bedroom. I love my books, wish I could just sit down and read them all. I found a book Lisa gave me in 1995. I wrote things in it for her, thinking when I died she would read it, but of course that never will happen. I find what I wrote 13 years ago even surprised me. I did have some insight back then, when I did not think I had any.

But it has taught me one thing reading it now, tell people now, talk now. I wished I had told Lisa Jean what I wrote for her and shown her. Then it still would have been there in the book for her later on. One thing I wish is that people would take and share more. For example, I will say something, they listen, but I don't get anything back. I feel like I am missing something, everything is "surface". I want to go deeper.

Example, talking to my sister on the phone. She told me a story of a cow. A man she knows bought some cows, some 25 miles from this home. He took them home, the next day one was missing. The cow during the night walked home to her own barn. So the man went back and got it. He said, he regretted that. He wished he had let the cow stay there as it had walked so far. I said to myself, well if he regretted it his whole life, why didn't he just to bring the cow back at some other time? I said to Jackie, I wonder why the cow went back, maybe it had a baby or another cow there who is now an adult that was it's baby. I wanted to know the reason for the cow's behavior. She just brushed that off, as not important to her it seemed. I brought up that question again. She was not interested in it. I wanted to talk more about in in depth, so that was that. After saying, wow, the cow walked 25 miles to go home, but why? I say to her, "see how smart they are, that is why we should not eat them, Jackie laughs and says something like this, "but prime rib or whatever is so good eating and she laughs. I say, you always laugh about it, thinking laughing makes it right. So she says to me, "then do what you want, don't eat it then." So that was it, but whenever I talk to her it seems, laughing makes it ok to her. I then told someone else the story, blah, blah, blah, not the laughing bit, but I say see, maybe we should not eat cows. I get no response, only that they listened and agreed how smart cows really are, but no feedback on the issue or response to me about eating them. It's disappointing. It would be nice if there was more conversations going on back and forth on a subject a person might bring up to another person. But I do understand, laughing or changing the subject is a way to print getting into a conflict or heated argument, so I get it.

May 25

It's been so long since I wrote in this journal, months. Now my desk is in the extra bedroom which has become my sanctuary. The only thing in the room that does not belong is the tv. The room contains my books, tarantulas, my little anoles, my desk, the spare bed, my altar, paints, a reading chair. What brought me back to my journal is a dream. I am going to put it in my dream book, and that is when I came across this journal.

Life has been terrible busy. Jackie sold her home and will move to PA. to be with her son Greg in July. Its so beautiful at her son's place. She will love living there. Tigerlily is leaving us for a nice riding farm in Rehoboth. Jimmy from Seekonk Oil bought her and we can go see her anytime at all. Plus the stipulation is when no one wants her I can get her back if I want. Zoe Jean is back at her dads, the stepmom moved out. Her life is better and life goes on. My heart aches for Lisa Jean.

June 1

Just woke up, nice time to write. Everyone is still sleeping. On that diet by blood type, I lost almost ten pounds, but up a little today from eating chocolate cake last night.

Jackie was over for supper last night. Zoe Jean has a baby bird and its doing fine. So good news, when Jackies leaves I am taking over her cooking stand. It will be a big help. Just got to get stocked up with supplies. Now Jimmy is not buying Tigerlily, but I think I have a buyer. A man at the post office hired me to do a stained glass picture. Its a dragon, its huge, 3 feet by 5 feet. I got it all leaded now I just need to paint it.

June 14
Tigerlily went to the farm today, she will be much happier there surrounded by children. It's close by, and we can visit her anytime and Zoe Jean can go on the weekend and work and ride for free. Destiny came by with her friend on their way to Cambridge to end her friend's pregnancy. Cannot tell someone else what to do, but feel its a shame, someday she will realize. Zoe Jean gets her new puppy next weekend. She is thrilled, the puppy is so cute.
Today we are going to Trevors party for graduation at his girl friends house. Trevor is all grown up! Well everyone is fine, cats are great, life if great except for my Lisa.

June 18
Nice day, rained late afternoon. Plants are growing like crazy. Bamboo is doing great. I met a friend on myspace, Pam, she is a awesome artist. Been having a great time chatting with her. I hung up some of my art in this room or mine. I took down the door. I hate doors, they take up so much space. Hung up new curtains and put one on the closet opening. I love having this room, its my own space. I also put up the art easel with my lion dream painting. I am trying to get into it again. There is never enough time to do it all. I want to read, paint, make rugs, garden, piano and play with Zoe Jean, and stained glass too. And I keep thinking of things to do. I want to fix the shed, take down the fence, move the plants, fix up the porch and on and on.
Oh, yeah I found a nice daisy plant growing in the middle of the yard and a bachelors button. See, its great when you don't mow the lawn. Natural and awesome plants will grow. I hear a tree frog in my pond!!!

June 19
Jackie is on her way back from Pa. I dreamed of Lisa last night, hugged her and heard her say "Lisa".

June 24
Zoe Jean is here, her dad is picking her up soon. The new puppy is great, very good. Yesterday I got my paints, will go to Jackies and work on my stained glass dragon. Its so big I am doing it on her dining room table.
Its raining out, we got some hail and nice lightning. Zoe Jean took off her clothes and ran out in the rain. Greg is getting a movie tonight. I got the book, the Artists Way, Pam the girl I met on Myspace told me about it. That book says to have a morning page you write everyday but I already do this with this journal. Its suppose to help to open your creative flow by writing it all down and not the non-essential stuff and getting rid of it.

June 25
I am going to try to write every morning. I started to do my books and almost forgot. Nice day out, but we have been getting rain every day. Are we going tropical?
Yesterday it was quite severe, hail and it was cold. A tree was ripped out of the ground near Greg's truck.
I think Zoe Jean will do fine by herself at home, her dad is back to work. The cats need their claws cut, Baby had a hard time jumping into the tub today but she ended up doing it. I wonder why she

does that. Greg brought home a great movie last night, the Bucket List.

June 29

Humid and hot today. Zoe Jean slept late and now is playing in the little pool on the deck. She has a frog in it and is now trying to catch a fish. The little puppy, Kubo is so sweet. He falls asleep on your chest. Last nights gig was awesome. Jackie went too. We sat at the table right next to Greg. Destiny and her friend stopped by to see the puppy. Joey is flying today. I might be fighting off a cold, the gland under my chin is sore. Today I made a super soup, I used the asian rice noodle bowl and added a can of chicken broth, some chicken breast, parsley and some curry. It was so good. Something funny happened today while I was folding my clothes. A hanger fell behind the washer, but I saw it from the corner of my eye. So it had to lift over the pipe it hangs on to fall to the back. If It was loose it would have fell straight down onto the dryer, not over behind the washer. Sort of weird. Greg is going to take Zoe Jean roller blading and Jackie and I are going to a farm stand to see if she can get another cooking account. I finished my meditation essay and got a 98.
Greg is practicing a new song and sounds so good. It will be nice when he is ready to play it out.

July 1

Summer is here. Its beautiful outside Zoe Jean is sleeping, the puppy is outside. We watched the new Rambo movie, it was really good. I bought fifty crickets yesterday, they are all chirping. Zoe Jean bought a Pac-man toad. A man bought three alligators. I took his picture, I wonder what he will do when they get big. He will probably get eaten, it's scary.

July 3

Jackie and I are going to deliver her apple squares to Marie's and I am putting in some stained glass pieces. Got up early today at 6 am, its the only way to get things done.
Yesterday went to the reading at the Angel Loft with Destiny, it went well, contact with at least six spirits.
My mom and dad came through, said my dad was short as Dennis came through too as the taller man. Dennis said he watches Destiny play cards and not to lose too much money and that he was very proud of her and that he is with her. My mom is around me. Derek came through and said he was sorry to Destiny and to me. She said he took his own life by substance abuse, but he was in a cloud so not aware when he did it. Then Shawn came through, she described him as lighter and broad shouldered. Lisa came in, said in a humorous way Destiny was a pain in the ass, but she is with her. Also that in her room there is a artistic picture. Destiny has a picture of her in her bedroom. Lisa said it is there and to hang it up. Derek is a teacher in the light and Lisa is a healer. Also Dennis said he was glad for me in my relationship. Destiny has it all on tape.

July 7

A overcast and rainy day. We have had rain everyday it seems. We are getting tropical for sure! But now I see the sun poking through the leaves. Jackie had a cookout yesterday I have had swollen glands for a few days and my tonsils hurt. The puppy Kubo is so precious. The Blue Jay escaped last week. Zoe Jean is being a brat about it and blaming me. She seems like she might be a little problem as she gets older. I hope she does not go through all that teenage crap. The flowers at the cemetery look fine and are all getting bigger. They buried someone behind Lisa last week. I saw deer tracks near her grave. The dragon painting is almost finished.

July 8

Nice sunny day and its hot. Everyone is sleeping. I wonder why I always wake up early. I have a cold still and a doctors appointment at three. Zoe Jean's dad is picking her up. That saves me a trip. Last night we watched a movie that greg picked up. It was funny. I love watching movies. Zoe Jean is not a little kid anymore, she made a card, a gift box and a present with wrapping paper for her boyfriend. She is very creative. I am going to take a picture of it. She is also more demanding and argues. I hope she does not go through a terrible teenage thing. She gets moody, but I guess that is her age. I think I will get Santoros pizza for dinner for Wed. I am going to make apple squares and cookies for him to try. I hope he says yes and puts them in his restaurant. Destiny just called she is walking Charlie, then has work. She is such a smart girl and determined. Kumo slept on me last night while watching the movie, he is so cute. Well as I write this I have more things to accomplish. I have my painting of the tigers set up and have not touched it in years, but its here waiting. I did fix up my workroom downstairs. I have done three pieces for the craft store in Mansfield, an owl, a angel, and a dinosaur. I also wrote the children stories I always wanted to publish. That will be fun. I might look into one that you pay, but I should look at publishers first. It seems everything takes so much time and effort. The cats are sitting around. They are so much company. I got to get going with my day.

July 9

Yesterday at the Doctors, got the results of my bone density test, and said I have Osteoporosis, mostly in my spine an a little in my hip. He put me on some meds. I don't think I am going to take them, side effects. I am going to try this stuff Ezorb for six months and do the test again and see what happens. It has no side effects. I am also on meds for throat infection. I feel ok. Today I cook for Santores. Its nice out and sunny. Zoe Jean went home yesterday. She is going to get checked out for braces July 29th, I am taking her.

Aug 3

I have been very lack at writing this journal. I love doing it but everyday flies by. We lost Angel our cat yesterday. She swallowed string, it was wrapped around her tongue and got her intestines all bunched up. They did surgery, but it was no good. She had about twenty holes in her intestine and they stitched it. I visited her on Friday at the hospital, she was glad to see me and purred quietly but she ran a temp and they called us on sat. Greg and I went down to see her and we were with her when they put her to sleep. It was so sad. But she was very distressed and probably would not live long and die very painfully. If only humans were so kind to each other. I buried her next to Kicho and put Daisys in the bottom of her grave and on top, also bee balm. Inside the towel she was wrapped in I put mom's purple phlox.
Last night I had a dream, I think it was about her. I am putting it in my dream book.

Today Joey has his helicopter show and cookout. Greg and I are going, maybe Jackie too. Zoe Jean is going to her grandmothers. Jackie has decided to move in with us. This is great news. We love her so much.

August 4
Greg and I went to the drive-in, it was fun but uncomfortable in the car. Funny thing, Kumo was barking out on the deck, barking down the steps onto the patio, at nothing! He kept doing it like something was there. Then he would lay down and stare with his ears perked up. He kept doing this. I wonder if Angel was there in spirit. Kumo did that when we first got him too. Down celler he all of a sudden looked toward the corner and got all upset barking. Spirits? Zoe Jean slept over her grandmothers, I am picking her up at 9 and today she is going to the horse barn to work, ride and have fun. I hope she likes it, it will be good for her.

October 18
Wow, its been awhile since I wrote in the journal. Cannot believe life is so busy. Zoe Jean never went to the horse barn to work. I started a "cookie route" now I have been doing it for six weeks. Its does really well. I have about 24 stops and usually sell our 200.00 each week. So its two days of cooking and one day on the road.
Jackie's sale of her house fell through. The people were jerks. But I think she will sell it. Destiny moved to Brockton. She is now only twenty minutes from her work. Her apartment is awesome. Its really nice. Destiny is such a hard worker. Joe is fine, he met a girl from Ohio, Joy, she came and stayed a month, but Joe likes being by himself and she went back to Ohio.

Moona the cat, had her babies. Three of them but one was born dead, a little black one. But she has a white one and a orange one. Now they are walking all over the house. There were born September 8th.

Kumo stays here with me, he is doing really good turning into a nice dog.

Well one more final on my Core Energy class and I have completed the four introduction classes. Now I will be able to choose my own subjects.

October 29

Its cold and clear outside. I cooked yesterday and will do more today. I went to Zoe Jeans house it was her Dad's birthday, I made the cake, her grandmother was there too. I took Zoe Jean to Walmart for things she needs and a halloween costume. The kitchen floor at the apartment got done today, Friday the rug will be done. I hope I get someone nice to rent it. I miss Lisa Jean so much! I can't believe this. Lisa my heart.

Jackie arrived in Florida on Monday. She is happy and cooking, I like cooking a lot too but keep thinking about a real job. Plus I would not be eating so much if I stopped cooking. No wonder all the chefs are fat. :-(

It seems like I never have anytime left now. No time for anything, but I do a zillion thins in one day, still so much more I want to do. Oh, if we could only go back in time I could hold you once more. We had so much to still share in our lives, so much to talk about. So many teas, or sitting on your front steps. Maybe going to Disney again. I loved it so much. I was so proud of you taking me to such a beautiful hotel. I can never thank you enough. How to live and go on, why is this like this? We live an die and lose the ones we love. I miss you Lisa.

November 14

Zoe Jean and I went to see Greg play out tonight. Trevor and his friends were there too, we had a great time. Destiny and family also came. Maureen is coming over tomorrow and we are going out again to see Greg play. Life is going by fast, keeps me so busy. But the reason I am writing is that at last I have some hope. Greg told me his dream last night and it was so vivid. At one point in the dream he thought he might be watching a movie, it was so real.

He told me it was a dream with Lisa there, but her not her body but her soul, and strange buildings. Jackie and myself were there too. There was a lot of crying but it was about whether if Lisa came back, not to stay but to only visit, it would be worth the grief and pain to see her, but only to have to let her go again. It was a dream of great conflicts.

I think about this, and I said it to Lisa, yes, its worth the pain, to see her and talk, we never got to say our goodbyes, its worth everything to me! Now its like waiting for spring. Maybe she will come. I now have some hope. It would be just like Lisa to ask Greg what he thought and how it would affect me if she came back. I know she is around. I was typing a address on the computer just the other day and somehow the keys got stuck, or whatever I looked and Liki" was in the address line. Almost her name. Plus she has melted angels with the candle wax for me. I would light a candle and tell Lisa to melt it for me, I would let it all burn down and on the plate would be a perfect angel outline of wax. I want her to know how much I love her. She is with me always. But with the dream of contact with Greg I feel great hope of seeing here. Sometimes I wish you could just dig up her grave, just to see her for real. She is truly my heart and soul.

December 30
Well life is flying by, its been awhile but I made a list of things to do everyday and writing in my journal is on the list.
Since I last wrote, Joe and I drove to Florida, 20 hours and Joe is a great driver. It was really fun and I am glad we went. Jackie works so hard but loves it..
No Lisa yet, but the other day as I was walking into the bathroom, I thought I heard my cell phone ring. So I went to look at it, of course the time was eleven past the hour! To me it was Lisa saying "hello." Zoe Jean was here for Christmas Eve and Christmas Day She did not want to be home as her step-mother was coming over for Christmas Eve.

December 31
It's snowing, really a lot. I went to get Zoe Jean this morning at 10:30 am and made it all the way to Swansea and had to turn around and come home again. On the way there my windshield wipers broke on route 195, so I ripped off the broken one and drove with the passenger one working. Joe's work place put on new ones.. Greg is suppose to play out tonight. I wonder if it will get cancelled. New Years ever is big money for him to lose. Well, I came home. I am glad Zoe Jean will be here later, she will be dropped off. Joe is sick, I hope he feels better later on.

January 1, 2009

Happy New Years! Well nothing exciting, went to bed last night early. Zoe Jean fell asleep around eight while watching the movie "Tropic Thunder." Greg played out with another band, Zoe Jean was good yesterday, a little bratty, she gets into these moods. We could have so much fun if she could control her attitudes, but she has a lot going on and she is only twelve.

In Feb. it will be six years since Lisa passed. I cannot believe how time just keeps on going by so fast. I love you Lisa Jean, my sweet baby girl. At least I have so much to remember, oh how I love you. We have snow everywhere, more coming on Friday. Heaven our cat is sleeping on the window bench next to me. That is one of her favorite spots. She is Angels sister from the same mother but a year younger. She is my favorite first white kitty. She loves me very much. Moona's little kittens are brats. They make so much noise in the mornings I have to chase them around with the spray bottle. Of course by then I'm wide awake! Destiny is getting her settlement 16,000 but she has lots of bills. She should save for land in Florida. I wish we all lived there. It's so nice. Greg and I are going down in Feb. It will be so much fun.

January 2

It cold and the ground is covered with snow. We might get a little more today. Charlie, Destiny's dog spent the night as she went to the Casino. Charlie is good but a pain, he needs to get fixed, Kumo too. Zoe Jean is sleeping, today we are going swimming and then she is staying over her grandmothers. Greg and I are going out to eat. She'll be back on Saturday. Back to school for her on the 5th. Doing my books, and daily activities. Playing the piano, etc. We will see what 2009 brings us. Good and bad, gains and losses.

January 3

Got to sleep late last night. I caught the brat kittens, and Moona and put them outside. They make so much noise. I had to do it again just now and Skye is on the porch too. He runs about, up and down the hall. I don't know how Greg sleeps. Yesterday I took Zoe Jean to swim but the pool is closed until Jan. 13th. So we had lunch at the hotel, then I took her to her grandmothers. Greg and I went went to Lincoln Woods to play the slots. We ate at Johnny Rockets, it was fun. Got home and Greg felt sick, like he ate something bad. Of course I then feel sick too. I always seem to get sympathy aches like his back hurt last week and then my back hurt. Zoe Jean might come back and we will got out to eat with Destiny.

January 6

Yesterday and the night before I was sick. I think it was from eating the wrong types of food for my blood type "O." All day yesterday I ate correctly and lost over a pound and I feel fine today. By eating wrong the last few weeks I gained seven pounds. Terrible, never ever eat wrong. Today I am going to put in the glass in the apartment at Lisa's. I made a beautiful picture of grapes for the kitchen window. I will see Joe today and maybe go see Zoe Jean. I have paint today too at 2:45. I almost forgot. I was all set to take off! Barry's, gregs drummers wife, Janet passed away on Jan. 1st. Greg went etc the service last night. She has been sick a long time. Poor thing, colon cancer.

Not that bad out today, a lot of the snow has melted, but a storm is coming tonight.

January 18
What is a Wizard?
Quote: "Not someone who can perform magic but someone who can cause transformation. A wizard can turn fear in to joy, frustration to fulfillment.
A wizard can turn the time bound into the timeless." Deepak Chopra

Its snowing right now strong. The cats love sitting in the window watching the birds. I am going to do the final on my class, "Magical Etiquette". Cooking today and maybe swimming. The roads might be ok. Zoe Jean is here for the weekend. She is going to the dentist on monday. No school Martin Luthers Holiday.
Joe fixed the pipes on the porch, they leaked everywhere so he took them out. Joe is so smart he can do anything.

Jan 2
Yesterday I took Zoe Jean to school, she had slept over and I took her to the doctors. She has a ear infection, we got her meds and had breakfast. She will be back here tonight. She has been really good. Just two times I got gas with Zoe Jean, it was eleven miles, texted her last night it was 9:11. Its eleven miles to swimming. When I dropped her off last week after swimming the speedometer was 1073 = 11 Makes me think of Lisa! :-)

January 23
"The most beautiful thing we can experience is the mysterious. It is the source of all true art and science. (Albert Einstein)

Do not meddle in the affairs of wizards, for they are subtle and quick to anger.

Finished my Magickal Etiquette class got a 100 on the final.

Never doubt that a small group of thoughtful, committed citizens can change the world. Indeed, it is the only thing that ever has. (Margaret Mead)

January 28
Snowing out, no school for Zoe Jean. Greg went to get his teeth cleaned by Mary Ellen. She is almost finished with school. I might just stay in my PJ's all day. :-) Started my wizard class, "Wizards of History" it should be very interesting. So far I have finished these classes:
Wizardry 100 becoming an apprentice   grade 100
Technomagick 100 grade 92
Ethics of Maick 200 grade 98
Core energy practice grade 98
Magickal Etiquette grade 100
I feel good but have been feeling really sad missing my Lisa Jean. I get these feeling of Lisa, she feels so solid and right there, it overwhelms me and I cry. It almost takes my breath away. She is so real. I love you Lisa.

March 1
Received this from Juan Andrade:
Love doesn't make the world go around, it makes the ride worthwhile.

April 10

I can't believe its been so long since I wrote in this journal. Not like me, but then it is, I get so busy with the mundane things of life. Lets see, Zoe Jean has spent a lot of time with me. I drive her back an forth to school everyday for the past three weeks. Last week she went home but is here three or four nights a week. She says her step-mother has not been around. So she likes that of course being with her dad. It gives me a break from driving and as long as she is happy and doing well its fine with me. She is beautiful, I wish Lisa was her to enjoy her.

We got 8 white fluffy little Silky chickens. They are so cute. Their skin is black and they have the most fluffy white feathers. Spring is here and the crocus, and daffodils are in bloom. The cats love running in and out of the house, the dogs would rather be inside. In the morning me and Zoe Jean are flying to Florida to see Jackie, we will be be back Thursday night. Jackie will be back here In May. Also I got a book contract for "Duck and Spider". I signed a 7 year contract and they liked my illustrations, so I am in the process now of doing all the pictures for the book. Exciting! :-) I am taking my art books with me so I can finish them.

Zoe might go to School One for 8th grade. We went to see the school and she loves it, she took placement tests and she has to go there for one week to see if she really likes it and if she can handle the work. Her day to go see it is on Tuesday, I will go with her too. I am sure he will love it. It would be so good for her. Better work, lots of art, great hours 9-3 and on Fridays 9-1. Freedom of expression. Greg is fine, my love. He is so good. Sometimes I don't know why he puts up with me. :-) He is playing excellent, sometimes

I wish I could put a video of him in this journal. Well thats it for now. I got to get back to my wizard class. So bad to let the important things slip.
End of journal 2007-2009

Journal 2011
November 17

Its been such a long time since I wrote in a journal.
I had this feeling tonight after fixing dinner, which I did not really eat, as I was full from snacking. I just don't want to eat meat anymore. Why this urge again? As I brushed my teeth I think, why do I or anyone want to eat a dead animal? It does not make any sense at all. Let's pretend, oh! look! a dead animal, lets skin it and eat it. What would make you desire to do that? Which I have done plenty of times in my youth. And why does this keep popping up in my thoughts? Then to do it, its such a dilemma. I am the cook in the house full of meat eaters. I guess, as the shopper and cook I am in control of how much meat we buy. Lately it seems like too much. Lets see, breakfast is easy, not many eat it, except on Sunday when we make a big breakfast. Since Destiny and Jackie moved out, and so much has happened this past year, losing Jackie's son Greg in his house fire in January.
So for breakfast we can make pancakes, French toast, eggs, waffles. So lots to make without meat. Even oatmeal and cereal or bagels. Not too hard to do.
How about lunch, I could make grilled cheese, tomato soup, salads, Chinese dishes with no meat. I am sure I can think of more options. I don't think anyone would miss eating meat at breakfast or lunch.

But at dinner I think they would.
And then Thanksgiving, just forget it, we have to have a turkey but after that I will have to think of meatless dishes for nightly dinners. Lets see I am happy with veggies and potatoes, onions and mushrooms, then sauce with no meat and any asian dishes. Even eggs on toast make a good dinner some nights. So I will work on it, also veggie chili and fish some nights.

We lost Greg in Jan. The call went in at 1:11 A.M. chimney fire. Greg did not wake up. They found him next to his bed on the floor in his blankets. Too sad and terrible.
My sister was in Florida at the time, the police called her and she met them at the Deleon Springs Post Office where they gave her the bad news. Strange that I lost my Lisa Jean in the fire in 2003 and my sister, her son.

February 2012
February 11
Does anyone ever stop to reflect on what they eat and how it effects the "objects they are eating?
I remember growing up, or working in the Chinese restaurant, I never ever gave it a thought. It was just, oh we have chicken, beef, pork, shrimp, and so on. It was so normal.
But put yourself now in the "objects" place. I guess it would not be so normal. Fear fills the air, fright, nerves and anxiety. Our earth is surrounded by death, the death of innocent "objects." From outer space we must have a black aura. They say no such thing as anyone having a black aura, but if it was possible that is what we would be reflecting back out to the universe.

Imagine the fear we have like when we go to the dentist or a child getting a shot, or our fear of our own death.
Now imagine your in line at the slaughter house, its your turn to become food.
Fear, fear, fear, fear.

If your a religious person remember God said, thou shall not kill, but kill what? humans? Animals? Did he specify? Maybe he is waiting on us to just stop killing, any kind of killing, human and animal.
Jesus said to turn your cheek. We never turn our cheeks. We kill, kill, kill and kill and call ourselves kind.
We are still barbarians. We think we are good and kind, but we never think of the horrors going on to keep us fat and full.
Just step in line, its your turn to become food,
Fear, fear, fear, fear.
And maybe someday the tables will be turned.
Some advanced barbarian race will come upon us, reflecting death and say, "See Dinner" and we become the "objects" on their dinner plates.

March 15
Lots of people see colors and swirls so this is not weird, but it is is what I sometimes see.
A few night ago, bedtime before I go to sleep I can see things with my eyes shut. Sometimes like a purple fog like globs with uneven edges, soft and floating and then they get smaller and smaller and then disappear, then another one appears and does the same thing. These I can see sometimes even if I open my eyes and then it disappears in a brighter white light. But the other night before sleep

I could see structures from above, like I was looking down on it, yellow and beige colors, not buildings but city like, but like it was made from stone or something like that. I kept trying to see it better, but the things I saw always seem to fade in and out. I did not see any vehicles or life. But one thing really surprised me is in one scene it had like a bridge and I could see under it, and as I was looking at it, (now remember, what I was seeing, there was no movement, no life) then all of a sudden there was a shadow on the ground moving around, it took me by surprise, and then it faded out again. Today, thinking about it, it came to me that the shadow could have been a plane? And I was in it looking down. The landscape I saw was not from this planet. It almost made me think of catacombs, but more square. This scene I had never seen before. I was not asleep when seeing any of this.

November 21
Dream: I dreamed of being in a park involved in selling stuff from a tent, like I do with Destiny, but in a park I did not recognize anyone I knew. It got very windy and we had to hold onto our stuff. Then after we all cleaned up the mess. Then I guess another day I helped set it up again. Everyone was helpful, but I do not know any of the people in that dream.

Its important to keep a dream journal even if the dream is short or does not make much sense. If you do save them, it will help you remember your dreams.

Lisa Jean

These are sayings I copied from one of Lisa's journals that I want to save.

One Spirit Journal, which was given to Zoe Jean on 1/9/2009

"Truth without compassion is hostility." (unknown)

"Will my actions here contribute to the peace within me and around me?"

"Be honest with yourself about what your values are.
Make your life a statement of what you love, believe in and respect." (John Robbins)

"Compassion, in which all ethics must take root, can only attain its full breath and depth if it embraces all living creatures and does not limit itself to mankind." (Albert Einstein)

"Cowardice asks the question, is it safe? expendency asks the question: is it politic? Vanity asks the question: is it popular?
But conscience asks the question: is it right?
And there comes a time when one must take a position that is neither safe, nor politic, nor popular, but one must take it simple because it is right." (Dr. Martin Luther King Jr)

"The opening of the trunk: The moment of inner freedom when the mind is opened and the infinite universe revealed and the soul is left to wonder dazed and confused, searching here and there for teachers and friends." (Jim Morrison)

"If the doors of perception were cleansed, everything would appear to man as it truly is, infinite." (William Blake)

"How should it be? Things are as they are, and I have a choice about how I react to them. I choose the life that I have right now, my actions are my only true belonging. I cannot escape the consequences of my actions, my actions are the ground on which I stand." (Shakyamuni Buddha)

"We can learn a lot from crayons. Some are sharp, some are pretty, some are dull some have weird names and all are different colors but they all have to learn to live in the same box".

"Love your enemies, bless them that curse you, do good to them that hate you, and pray for them which despitefully use you and persecute you." (Jesus, an extremist for love)

"Do not follow where the path may lead, go instead where there is no path and leave a trail." (Howard Pollock"

"The strong do what they have the power to do and the weak accept what they have to accept." (Thucydides)

"Hatred never ceases by hatred in this world. Through doing kindness it comes to an end. This is an ancient law."

"Devoid of stars, darkness cannot drive out darkness: only light can do that. Hate cannot drive out hate: only love can do that."

(Matin Luther King Jr.)

I love you all the way to stupidity by Zoe Jean said to her mom, meaning to say, I love you all the way to infinity."

To Zoe Jean
"I want to hold you in love and light so you may feel my arms outstretched around you.
Rest my love in these arms, may my love be a catalyst for your growth.
May the love we share reside in your heart.
May you wake in the morning with vitality and meaning.
May you know how much I care for you and that you are in my heart."
Written by Lisa Jean for Zoe Jean

To Zoe Jean

Zoe Jean
"Someday I will teach you, my little one how to stand up tall, how to be proud, and how to be your own person.
Living my life, trying to see myself through your innocent eyes, how what I do today will affect you tomorrow. I know how you will do as I do, not as I say, trying to detoxify my life of negativity now before it reaches you."
Written by Lisa Jean for Zoe Jean

Zoe Jean
"My girls getting so big! Seven months old today, wow!

Seems like yesterday you were a little peanut. Now your starting to move around in your walker. Making lots of new noises, like bob-bob-ba and something very close to mom. Your favorite toy is your red frog. And you Love it when I dance you around the house and kiss you. Your giving big kisses, or trying to eat my face, and are a cuddle bug. A couple of weeks ago you started crying whenever you see me. I must hold my baby at all times and your reaching out your hands for me to pick you up. You are also eating small foods. You have started doing so may new things in the past few weeks but no matter what you do I'll always love you." xoxo Lisa, mommy

Before Zoe was born Lisa wrote:

"Anticipating your arrival, waiting and wondering so many questions running through my mind, what you'll look like, and how I'll kiss you from head to toe. Wrap you up and warm you with my love, keep you safe and secure in my arms. Can't wait to welcome you into the world. I want to be a great mom. I love you so much already. Just a image in my mind, a little princes inside."

A little thing Zoe Jean said to me when she was two years old. She likes to pretend that she is a dragon. One day she was very upset, so to cheer her up I asked her if her name was dragon woman. She said to me in a very sad voice, "don't call me dragon woman, my name is dragon cry."

My Grandmother

My grandmother, Ruth Bolton wrote poetry and was an artist, played the piano, raised six children on a farm. When she was five she was taken by her school teacher to Mass. from Tennessee, and was never returned. Her real name was Rose.
These are some of her poems, and she used the pen name Phebe Robinson.

No Answer

Dear little bird, bright as a flower.
Happy ever in sun or shower.
How did you know that spring was springtime,
Up here in the north?
Why did you come winging back
Across the wide sky's endless track,
Back to the tree you loved the best,
Back to last year's dear home nest?
Did some distant star's pearl light
Guide you safely through the night?

Bright little bird in your leafy bower
Why so secure in your green tree tower?
Is it because heaven is so near
That there is nothing at all to fear?
Or, could you know that the God of all
Marks the little sparrow's fall,
And rest in simple trust, content,
Up there near the firmament?

Happiness

I may not learn the music of this life
In measure full,
But running through the day,
Be it gay or long,
There is a sweet refrain,
A lovely song,
Persistent, yet elusive,
With often times a lull,
Which long continued makes the spirit numb,
The senses dull,
But when I reach that heavenly plane,
And there perfected it will be,
Merged in heaven's symphony.

Spring Ploughing

Neighbor says its early to be ploughing up the farm,
But my heart is full of courage and the air is full of balm,
The red-headed woodpecker is hammering hard
On the old pear tree in our back yard.
He is playing taps for the winter's storm,
And the sun is making the earth right warm.
Anybody knows it must be Spring
When the little red robin starts to sing.
The brown ribbon turns on a graceful curve,
And I watch my mark lest I should swerve,

And the breezes murmur, "Summer's on the way".
So I keep on a ploughing the live-long day.

The Hero's Son

My love was lost in the battle grim
But you look at me with the eyes of him,
And your every gesture gives me joy
Though you are such a little boy!
Your shoulders sway and your step is sure,
You're my lost love-in miniature.

Day Dream

The trees down in the orchard
Were feeling very gay,
And I thought as I was passing
That I heard one of them say,
"I think you are a Pippin
Standing there so straight and tall".
And the answer, "You're a little peach,
And that's not saying all".
And then a tree beyond me
That had tried the sky to reach
Tossed its leaves and murmured,
"I wish I were a peach".
And then the Spy who was standing by, said
"Whatever goes or comes
You're the best one of us all,

For you get all the plums".
Then they shook their tiny leaves
And laughed a silvery chime
For the trees were feeling very gay
In the warm, sweet summertime.
And I hurried down the shady path
Until I found the stream,
And I wondered if I'd really heard,
Or was it a daydream?

A Song Of Northfield

Chimes of music from the Chapel
Peal out on the evening air
Breaking through the peaceful silence
Of our Northfield Campus fair.

And the light from Stone Hall gleaming
Sends its rays through darkest night
Keeping watch upon the Campus
Till we wake to morning light

Though our founder, wise and noble,
Sleeps on younger rounded hill,
Absent in the body from us,
Yet his spirit dwells here still.

Honer to his hallowed memory
Praise and love we gladly pay

He trusted in the ancient promise
I will keep it night and day.

Chorus

Hail to Northfield! Hail to Northfield!
She has taught us life anew.
Hail to Northfield! Hail to Northfield!
And to her we're ever true.

People, Problems and Bitching

Is it just me or what? People drive me crazy sometimes. For example, someone will tell me all about a problem they are having, and so on and so on and so on. Then after listening I have some good suggestions, but its like they do not even want to address it, like yeah, that might work or be a good idea and then talk about it, but it seems they are not looking for an answer they just want to vent. To me its a waste of my time, why tell me all this stuff if I cannot contribute to maybe a solution? To me that is frustrating, so I have learned to mostly listen and say, oh! wow! that sucks, and then they still like to complain about it again and again.

Oh, but tell them a problem you are having, and its like calm down, or they go into something that might have happened to them like that, but then it turns into some issue they had and what you were talking about is not even on the plate anymore.

Another thing is people talking about politics, I have no interest in it, I don't even care, I think people are crazy listening to it at all. Your only here a short time and soon will be dead, so unless you can resolve a issue what is the point? You can complain and complain, but it seems the only thing you can do that might change anything is to vote, write to the officials etc, and even that sucks. Join the best group to do the right things, but its seems no one can do the right things enough to make everyone happy, no matter what they do, someone does not like it. And if you did save the whole world but you were not on their team in politics, they still hate you and say you did nothing. I cannot live in that world, its not my world. Politics is a whole separate bubble. So why get all stressed out on what those people are doing. It makes no sense. I try to live a peaceful life, do the right things for people around me and hopefully it goes forward into the world. To me, its pointless to talk and talk about what this politician did or did not do, or what people are saying they are going to do, and its just crazy.

I use to listen to it all on the news and get all involved, and all it did was make me angry and stressed out. I do not listen to it anymore, by doing that it really changes your life. You even sleep better. Shut it all off and live a decent life. I would love to change the things going on in the world that is not moral and so wrong, but I can't, I can only influence what is right around me and teach others by how I act.

Then what is it with people driving today, no one seems to show any respect on the road, they all act angry. There is so much road rage. People have killed people right in our own state over it, so is this a dribble down from people listening to political news and how angry people are towards others who are not sharing their viewpoints? People are stressed out, it has to be coming from somewhere.

Then what about people who never really listen to anything you say? You know the song by Led Zeppelin, Living Loving Maid, She's Just A Woman? Right, I was listening to the words and in one particular section, it hit the nail right on its head.

"Nobody hears a single word you say

Living, loving, she's just a woman

But you keep on taking till your dying day

Living, loving, she's just a woman."

Now I am relating this to me telling someone something, so it fits perfectly.

And I am not talking about those annoying women who really never ever shut the fuck up. The ones you would like to smash, but you don't you just have to say, excuse me, I have to go do something, or hide from them, you know the kind I mean? So that is why it is like, you can talk and tell someone something, but they are not really listening, even though they say they are. Cause I know, they might have listened to some of it, but later they will always ask a question, and should know the answer cause you already told them it. And even later when you tell them a second time, sometimes they come back again with the same question. WTF!

This happens so much that I am really surprised when someone does something like, for example my son brought me home a lemon cake, that put me in shock, like he really paid attention that I loved lemon, when that happens I am totally surprised that someone took the time to pay attention. So am I a total bitch or is this something that relates to you?

One other thing I can think of while I am on the subject is how about when your at a social function, and you and another person are talking about stuff, it seems like a good back and forth conversation, but then someone or something happens that interrupts the conservation, and if I happened to be the last person in the middle of the conversation, when the interruption is over, the other person just either never says oh, yeah, and gets back into the conversation, it just ends, so you never get to finish. When that happens the other way around, I always let them continue their thoughts. So you end up walking away, like ok why did I even come to this party to socialize in the first place when everything is so superficial. I am not going to stand around and pretend this is so much fun.

And then how about parties for kids, that was never my thing in my whole life. There is nothing worse then a party where all the adults are standing around watching all the kids run around and think they are the most adorable things. And try to talk to this new generation of people with kids, unless its about their kid you might as well go get a drink. I think back in the day, things were different when adults went out to hang out. I never remember people being rude in a conversation. And when the adults got together, it was adult time, the kids were told to go play. They were not allowed to hang around and listen to the adults talk.

We did all kinds of good things with our kids, fishing, cooking, trips to the library, vacations, I taught them everything, piano, how to build things, have pets, catch bugs and frogs. It was so much fun having kids. But adult time was just that, kids not included. Today it seems different. If your talking to a parent, and a kid interrupts, the parent it seems just goes into another zone, the kid just took over, and when the parent is done with them, they never look back at you and continue what you too were talking about, no matter how much it seemed they were interested, even when it was all about something they were doing etc. We taught our kids not to interrupt, if they did they were told not to, and had to wait, unless it was important they could say excuse me, and then I would listen.

Certificates Etc

A few things that I have accomplished that are meaningful to me. I finished one year of classes at Dean Jr. College in Franklin, MA. I majored in Math/Science. I loved it but work and raising two children was enough on my plate. I wish I had finished as I enjoyed it so much. I did get accepted at a Nurses school, but they did not have any financial aid at the time and I could no afford it.

I did one level of the Dr. Edward Bach Foundation Distance Learning Program. My daughter Lisa Jean completed the four year course and was a Master. Learning about flower essences and how they can help with our emotions was and still is a important craft to know. You can buy the Bach Remedies at many stores and online.

I was also a UFO Field Investigator for Mufon for a couple of years. I held meetings at my home. It was very interesting and met many nice people. And now they came out with so much information, that congress held a special meeting and told about the UFO sightings.

I took a course from the Project At Earth Academy. It was based on the book by Nancy Malacaria, Earth Sister.

This is an outline of the book: The Project At Earth Book One- September 1, 2006.

Saturday, May 12, 1990 began an ordinary day for an ordinary Massachusetts couple, Jack and Nancy Malacaria. But this day would mark the beginning of an ongoing and incredible revelation that would transform their lives, and Earth, forever. Jack and Nancy soon began to speak through the UFO field and public media to openly share what they learned through their thousands of personal experiences with the alien races, and to help other experiencers get to know their own alien contacts. Now read Nancy's daily journals to experience their journey for yourself-an intriguing true account of the introduction and progression of their family's relationship and education with the leaders of the organization of the 218 alien races visiting Earth.

I see this book is available on Ebay by the author.

Besides the certificates, I have been writing books, mostly children books, a cookbook, a childhood biography and some books on prison art and Covid-19 in prison. I am working on new books all the time. Please check them out on Amazon, Barnes and Nobles, Thrift Books, Sure Shot books and probably other sites.

The bio on the authors page:

About the author: I was born and raised in Massachusetts. I have three children, a granddaughter and lots of pets. I won Miss Franklin when I was two.

I love to collect rocks and gems. I love music and play the piano, guitar, and I try to play the didgeridoo and the Native American flute just for fun. I make my own alien creatures with clay and cook them in a kiln. I also like to paint dragon eyes on rocks. Sometimes you might find my daughter and me at a local art festival with our crafts. I also love to cook.

I am a vegetarian in progress and an animal advocate.

I love writing books for children and also books about cats, art and inmate stories. I illustrated my first book, Duck and Spider but the other books were illustrated by talented people who are in prison, such as Original Dragon Art From Within The Dungeons Across America, Dinner at Dragon's House, The Flower That Wanted To Dance, The King's Journey, Two Hungry Bears, Build Your Own Squirrel Proof Bird Feeder, Change the World Cookbook and The Great Cooking Contest. Henry and Sara was illustrated by my daughter Destiny Jean and written by her sister Lisa Jean. Secret Friends was illustrated by Destiny Jean also. I am in the process of writing more stories, and the newest one is Within the Gates Of Hell, True Covid-19 stories written by inmates. I illustrated the cover on that one. I designed the cover with creatures I made for,

Are You A Hoarder? Then the other books are done with photos of cats, Tabitha a True Story, The Tabitha Tree, Dragon Eyes and Skye. The bio of my childhood, What It Was Like When I Was Little. https://amazon.com/author/stardragon135

I have been creating my art at Red Bubble. You will see it on many items such as T-shirts, clocks, rugs, shower. curatins, notebooks, cards etc. If you would like to check it out you can at:

stardragon135.redbubble.com

I have been awarded two certificates from my clients, one is a Golden Heart Award and reads: Humanitarian doesn't describe how awesome you are, with a heart of gold, your compassion, hope and generosity keeps touching the lives of perfect strangers. Thank you for being a difference maker. The 2022 Golden Heart Award is presented to Barbara J. Nagle Our dear Dragon Lady.

The Golden Dragon Award 2023 reads: This award is presented to Barbara J. Nagle (Stardragon) Whom with her golden heart, cheerful soul, wise advise and a helping hand, is truthfully the Golden Queen of all misunderstood dragons across the Nation. Thank you for your services!!!

Extra

I was always interested in the movies and how awesome it must be to be involved with the filming of one. So I got my lucky day as an extra in the movie, Bleed for This with Miles Teller and Aaron Eckhart, a true story about a boxer from Rhode Island. It was awesome and so fun to see the action take place.

Simba

Its June 3, 2024, and I saw a memory on FB that we lost our Simba on that date but in 2023. When I saw that I could hardly believe that it has been a year since he was here. How could that be?
Just the other day Destiny and I were driving down route six and drove right by the vets where I had to take him on his last day.
As I looked over at the parking lot, I just relived my last moments holding him in the parking lot all over again, asking him if it was ok. He confirmed it was by looking right at me and blinking then taking a deep breath. As I sit here writing this, tears streaming down my cheeks, I am just as heartbroken today as I was then.
So I found the sympathy card the vet sends with you when you leave with your now dead pet. The card says, "Life with your friend was like no other, and the memories are your own, but as you say your last goodbye, just remember you are not alone."

From Bay State Veterinary Emergency and Specialty Services. They included a little packet of Simba's fur, and some cards with his foot prints on them. On the front of the card they made a little bouquet of flowers with the stems wrapped in Simba's bandage.

I also got in the mail a card from his regular vet, and that one had a little cat shaped felt cutout that was filled with seeds that you are suppose to plant in memory of your cat. I did not do that last year, I am going to do that today.

The card says this: When you plant this kitten adornment in your garden, wildflowers will bloom year after year in memory of your much beloved pet."

Dr. Truesdale and Staff.

Then my daughter, Destiny got me a card, flowers and beautiful wind chimes to remember Simba. On her card she wrote: "I am so sorry for your loss. Boo was such a strong brave cat and will always be with you. Love Destiny and Kevin xoxo

And then I got a beautiful card from Simba's Acupuncturist.

She wrote: "you did a great job in listening to Boo, and doing what he was asking you to do. It's so hard, he has left a huge hole, but his soul is at peace, only his body was lost. Your a great kitty mom! Love Deanna."

Everyone that we knew sent us heartfelt messages either by phone or on fb. So I have my little packet of these cards saved in a special place.

One of my favorite memories of him was how he would come walking into the living room, in a sassy strut, around the corner with his tail up and slightly swaying back and forth and I swear a wise grin on his face, his blue eyes looking up at me and Greg. He was a little wise guy. :-) Then he would love to play hide and seek,

I would take him out on the lawn, and set him down, I would give him a little push and I would run and hide behind a tree, he would come running and find me, and I would repeat that, he loved to play. I would do a magic show for Simba, his brother Skye and his sister Baby. I would say out loud, "magic show, magic show," and the three would come running, I would sit on the floor and they would sit in from of me. I had some of their toys and I would throw one up in the air and catch it in my hand then hide it behind my back, then bring it out like in a big surprise, oh! there it is! They would sit in front of me the whole time and watch this magic show. It was so cute. Good memories of the three, we still have Baby who is now 18 years old and is doing pretty good. We have been so honored to be able to share our lives with such a loving, wonderful cat family.

A nice response I got from fb:
Pyramid GodAnubis: it's ok we all know of Simba, know he was of a true Royal Stem and was amongst kings and queens with you and love and passion. His anniversary means a lot and is respected.

A Walk In The Woods Meditation

 As I look out my window this spring morning I notice that the sun is shining brightly and the wind is blowing gently. I can see the pine trees from my window and the sun shining down through them. It

looks so quiet and peaceful. I can hear the sound of my loved pets in the background, the quiet song of the chickens an occasional quack of my duck, and the happy bleating of my sweet little goats. I can see them looking towards my window with their bright eyes searching me out, hoping for a treat or a friendly rub. I have been working all morning and I think its time for a break. I grab a warm jacket and put on my boots. As I go out my door I grab my old worn walking stick I found last year. I glance back into the house and see my cats all sleeping peacefully. It's time to take my walk and relax. As I walk down the steps I see my fairy figurines have survived another winter and the spring flowers are coming up. As I walk down my path the animals are excited to see me and make a commotion as I walk by. Not today my friends, I am going on a walk. I leave my yard and head out into the swamp. As I go along I step gingerly looking for footing without getting my feet wet. Today I am going to find a way across. As I walk I can see the hawks flying over, drifting along so peacefully with wings outspread, just gliding along. I can hear some small birds singing their spring songs, and hear the crows cawing off in the distance. The tall brown grasses swish by me as I walk along using my walking stick for guidance. I am looking for frogs or turtles but see none. Soon I am out in the middle of the swamp, and in the center of the swamp is a big opening of grass forming a large circle. It seems as if I am in the center of the universe. I look up into the sky and see the clouds in the blue sky. It is so beautiful. I close my eyes and imagine I am the hawk drifting gently on the breeze, looking down at me. I would be a dot of color in the center of a huge field of grass and then the trees surrounding that. I am a million miles from anyone and I find peace. I smile to myself enjoying this vision and I feel the cool breezes on my face, the sun warming the top of my head. I open my eyes and begin walking again now onto the other side of the swamp to see what is there. As I go along I start to come to firmer ground and the pine trees await me with their tall beauty and the fragrant smell of the woods. Near this edge I find small skunk cabbages starting to grow, I lean over and pick one, loving the smell of it. A gentle skunk smell but so springy. Spring is here at last I think as I am looking around for more signs. I see the needles of the trees on the ground and little dug up holes from the squirrels. I look up into the tall trees and see their nests. Closing my eyes I imagine being up in that nest so far into the sky, swaying in the tree tops. I am so warm and cuddled next to my brother squirrel, watching the world below from so high. Over the tops of the trees is my view, the first to see the rise of the moon and the last to see the setting sun. I feel so at peace but I must go on and see what lies ahead. The ground starts to slant up a little and I find myself walking over trees that had fallen during the winter, old stones that have been here for zillions of years, touching the surface of them with my fingers, feeling for their memories, honoring their oldness. This early in the spring I don't see too much green life yet, but the woods are full of bright green moss. It covers the old stones, and the trunks of the trees, so golden green and bright. The gem of the woods. I then come across a beautiful old pine, perfect in strength and fullness. So tall and awesome, with its young, surrounding it here and there all trying to reach the sky. I go up to it and touch its smooth bark. I see pine pitch here and there, small balls of clear shiny gel. As I smell the pine trees fragrance, I lay my cheek up against its cool surface and feel its life within me. I wonder how old it must be, I am a babe in comparison. I move on and notice an area of soft pine needles surrounded by baby pines all fluffy with soft green needles. I grab a handful of its branches and pull it through my hands as I walk by. I love the coolness of them. I pick off a needle and bite into it, tasting the fresh piney taste. As I look at the bed of needles I feel a very strong desire to lay down on them. So I do, and stretch out on my back feeling the spongy layers of pine needles under me, and I look up into the tall trees, up through the branches with the sky peeking through so high up above me. The contrast of the dark branches and the bright blue sky. Then I shut my eyes and listen. I can hear the gentle wind swooshing through the tops of the trees, then I start to notice my breathing as it quiets down and I listen very quietly and I hear my heart beating, my life. Soon I hear the rustle of a little animal here and there. Maybe a chipmunk looking for food or burying a little morsel of food it found. I can still hear the birds singing, "spring! spring! Its here! Find me love! Lets have babies!" With my eyes shut I listen and drift off to sleep, so far from home, so far from humanity. The dappled sun on my face and hands. I sleep. Then I awake, everything is so quiet, the sun is setting as the woods grow darker I look up into the trees again, its now more dusky and to my surprise, as I look up I see the large eyes of an old owl looking down at me, blinking the way owls do. He sits there and looks at me for a long time. I notice his beautiful feathers, brown and black and the golden eyes so large. His curved yellow beak and strong claws on the branch. As I sit up, he looks at me one last time and flies off deep into the woods. Time to trek back home. I grab my walking stick, a little stiff from laying so long on the ground and head back. The trees casting long shadows, the sun slowly sinking down over the horizon. I hear the owls hooting in the distance. Time to hunt, watch out little mice. I come to the edge of the swamp, little pools of water here and there sparkling with the reflection of the late afternoon sun. Crossing over the swamp I think of coming back soon and seeing more life awakening in my woods. Maybe next time I will see Lady Slippers. I now hear the anxious bleating of my goats, waiting for their dinner, looking for their master to feed and love them. I am back in my world, glad to be back and glad to greet my lovely animals that I adore. I will feed and give love to my pets and poke around the yard, fix a board, repair a fence, enjoy, then put my walking stick back in the corner to wait for our next journey and thanking the spirits for this eye awakening walk in the woods.

Hugging

I was thinking about hugging and how it makes you feel good to get a hug from someone you love. They say its important. First I am going to say what I think about it before I look it up on google. I grew up in a loving family, but we were not huggers. So when I meet people that want a greeting hug or a goodby hug it was always weird. Because of not growing up in a hugging family I really do not want to touch other people. Like when and if I went to church, they have a moment when everyone turns around and greets the other people around them with a touch or whatever. If I went to a church that did that I was most likely not ever going back, and it was not because I am not a loving person, I am, but to me that is just plain weird. Now, hugs in a relationship are different, like giving your kids or boyfriend or husband a hug is great, or getting one. Now if I see a old friend, the first thing you do is give a hug, which is like if you don't that feels weird, but it still feels a little weird when you do, especially if you know them but not real good, its always awkward to me. But pets are different, we love them as family, so petting and or holding your pet always feels good. And you can hold or pet them a long time and its not weird. Then I see children as babies, they seem to have a favorite teddy bear or some stuffed animals, or a blanket they carry with them at all times. I see if they feel shy, they are hugging it tightly. I know adults call them security blankets or security toys. I think it is like a hug to them holding it close it makes them feel safe. I remember reading about cows going to slaughter, and it was a big problem to get the cows to walk in calmly to their deaths. They would panic and it caused a lot of delays in the great scheme of a fast smooth line, the faster the better, the more profits they can make. A woman, who had emotional issues, read about it, and knew something about feeling safe or how to feel safe. So she designed a Squeeze chute that would hold them tightly as they walked in it. It calmed the cows right down. So this is like getting hugged for a cow. We also see old people having a stuffed animal or doll to hold, and it seems to me woman have them the most, I don't remember if old guys do. But if I see a cute stuffed animal that reminds me of my pet, I will pick it up and hug it. It feels so good. At Christmas this year, I got a black stuffed cat, the kind you can put a heating pad inside. And you can hug it and stay warm. So I tried it, it is so comforting to hug something close to you, It relaxes you and makes you feel safe. After I lost my loving cat, Simba, it was also very comforting to hold it with or without the heating pad. It has little arms and you can hold its paw. I use to hold Simba's paw when I fell asleep with him next to me. So I was thinking that hugging anything will make you feel better, secure and maybe loved. So I think it might be a good experiment to say when you go to sleep grab something to hug, it could be a pillow or your blanket crumbled up close to you and shut your eyes. See how it feels, I think you will feel better. I think our brains do not distinguish between real and not real. We already know our brains believe what we tell it, that is why you never think or say things bad about your body, your brain has a way of making things happen that you might not like. Also the is why during surgery doctors are not suppose to joke around about the patient, like oh, he's going to die, or that gall bladder is bad, because they found out the person's brain can still hear what is being said, even though you are knocked out. If the brain hears negative things it is apt to not have a good outcome as opposed to hearing positive things. So give it a try, hug something it will make you feel better, it will give you a better feeling and outlook. It might not be a person your hugging but your brain is saying, "oh hugs, its so good" and probably releases good feeling hormones. Also if you are out and about and need a hug, or are thinking of a loved one you can just put your hands together and hold them tight over your heart, and think of that person or pet with love and don't feel sad, make sure you smile and think of happy times together. So now I am googling, why is hugging important. This is what shows up: In his famous and controversial experiments, psychologists Harry Harlow revealed just how important physical contact is for mental wellness. Hugs not only reduce stress, they also help increase happiness, boost immunity, reduce conflict, and improve over well-being. Why it is important to hug someone? Hugs lower your blood pressure and heart rate, while also improving cardiovascular function. Hugs decrease the release of cortisol, making you less stressed and allowing for improved sleep. Hugs boost oxytocin in our bodies, which is associate with feeling happier. What happens if you don't hug someone? When you don't get enough physical touch, you can become stressed, anxious, or depressed. As a response to stress your body makes a hormone called cortisol. This can cause your heart rate, blood pressure, muscle tension, and breathing rate to go up, with bad effects for your immune and digestive systems. When cuddling something soft and comforting and humanoid, levels of cortisol, a stress hormone are greatly lowered from physical contact. Alongside the, comfort releases oxytocin, a hormone that relaxes and soothes the mind. But research shows that stuffed animals do the same things for us. So you can google the same questions and get tons of answers with all about the same results. So grab something to hug. It will make you feel better, remember if its a person, make sure they want to hug too. Your favorite stuffed animal or pillow to will give you the same results because and maybe better as you don't have to ask and people tend to not want to hug for very long. I think we need to hug for a longer time, so when you wake up, or are going to sleep you can hug till you naturally fall asleep or in the morning till you feel good. I noticed that once you start hugging you really don't want to stop, it must be your body releasing good comfort hormones.

Dreams from Journals

I was outside and I remember running and then feeling my body lift off the ground as I ran. I did it twice, it felt so awesome I was flying. Then when I woke up I was so disappointed that it was not real. Then I dreamed about this dream again, but after flying I called my mothers house to tell her about flying. Dickie by brother answered and would not let me talk to her, as he said she was busy, and had company. I wanted to tell her about flying. I wanted to tell people but knew they would not believe me. Also I drove a truck to Star Market warehouse, and did not see anyone I knew. People had a town there set up like a fair. I met a woman and a kid. We went to get coffee, well, I got cocoa and used some change I had in my purse and put it on the counter with the other money to help pay.

I was dreaming early on this morning and I was in this building and there were lots of people working there. It seemed their job was to diaper a new baby. I remember bringing a baby to this older woman and telling her how to do it. She did a good job and the baby was happy. Then in the dream I had a horse to ride. He was all saddled, but I had to put on its bit, something was wrong with it, but I got it on. I was riding it out of the building, and then someone told me of a nice place to ride, an indoor garden, so this lady took me to this broken down old house. It was old and I rode through these little rooms, I could not find the garden. Then I rode past these old stairs something like attic stairs. Someone lived up there and their little ugly dog, like a bat face came charging down and started biting my horse's leg, it was tearing the flesh right off in chunks. I grabbed it by the head and gave it to the old woman who was the owner. The horse was ok. Then I woke up. I had a dream I was in the woods, in front of my mom's house, climbing the pine trees trying to do something or build something. There were some people in the driveway, standing by a car, one woman I knew I wanted to tell her about the flying dream but did not. Then I saw some kids going someplace like in the woods on a trail in a row like with a teacher. I thought one was Zoe Jean but it was not, I woke up very disappointed, not really flying. Another time I dreamed I was raking a friends yard, like half of it, and was going to mow the rest later. I also was moving something from a horse farm. Another time I had this dream I caught a huge catfish and put it in a tank. Then it seems like a man was there and was going to buy it, but he did not he said he would come back later. Then I was moving some daffodils from near the swing set and then another man stopped by and bought the catfish. It was huge and cost the man a lot of money. Then we were hearing how the catfish would change size and it would become very small. On another part of the dream I was riding a horse through the woods, somehow ended up in a swamp, went out onto the dirt road and met up with another group of people on horses. I was talking to two of them. The had too much baggage with them, and one man had a big bag of cheese snacks. I told him he should have got the crunchy kind as the bag is a lot smaller in size. In this dream a cat woke me up, then I realized I was dreaming. A very mixed up dream, in one part, a person gave us a book and I went to show Greg to look at it, it contained a spell written on one page. Some about a spell to irritate a person. I saw that I did not want the person who gave us the book to see it, but then on the next page was a video, it shows my daughter, she was doing a Indian dance in a circle, we could see the back of her, she could really dance well. Then at one point she shook her hips or something , she was awesome. Then it was over. On the way out, (we were in a barn or some sort of a building) Greg gave a bottle of wine to someone, and said we bought it, but it was really Lisa's, that made me so mad, that he did not say it was hers. Then as he was walking away I threw something at him, like pudding, well someone was standing behind him as he walked and it hit them instead. It went all over their head and face. Lol. I called the person over to me and they came up to me saying it looked like I was throwing it right at them, so I told them what I was doing as I wiped of off their face. When we were leaving, someone there said we should watch the Three Stooges with them. In another dream it's hard to explain for some reason I see a field, some hawks at the end of it, I need to get across it to escape? I go across it but get into some kind of animal pits filled with water and dead animals, I can't get out and there I dead fish too. I can't seem to find a better way out, It just keeps getting worse.

This dream I was at a resort of some sort, Skye was with me and was always sitting on my lab. When I was ready to leave I tried to walk back to my car through the cutout paths, but somehow could not, the tour bus said you had to use them to get back, and I did not know how to get on the tour bus. So I went back inside, from inside it was even more confusing. I talked to people but somehow I could not take Skye with me if I wanted to leave.

Went out to a gig and had this dream just before I woke up. I was in South America with Zoe Jean we were on the beach and it was really nice. There were weird rocks in the water, tall and they stuck up maybe two feet tall from the surface. Lots of people, and also a carnival was going on. So we go back to the hotel, she goes ahead of me and then I cannot find her. At the hotel which has pink stucco, I saw my cats are out and also puppy are outside. They come with me up the stairs to our room. I see the door is a old shower curtain, no wonder our pets got out. There is a old mattress on the floor and messed up blankets, and stuff all over the floor. It was a mess. I see a child sleeping under the blankets but its not Zoe Jean, but a girl her age. She says she has no parents, she has braces on her teeth, and I look at her teeth an they are very clean and I think to myself she is no stray. Then Zoe Jean and I are at this old ladies house. There is a priest there too. Up in back of the house is a church, but you cannot see it. Then some guy is across the street singing. Zoe Jean's dad is there, and he decides to go down back of the house in the field. He is wearing a black robe and I see he has his face covered in a black mask. He is singing, "I do not need a microphone". Then I am making soup for the priest and getting him some bread. Then we see the priest and people come down from the church, and they see Zoe Jean's dad. Well of course they think its evil and tell him to stop. Then I and the priest tell him even though its not evil but he has to stop as the old lady let us stay at her house and they might do something to her if you don't. Thats the way it is, but why was I even in South America?

This dream I had was of Lisa. Her cat work me up and ended it, but I remember some of it. We were in a store, Lisa met a lady and was talking to her. Lisa asked her name and the woman said: "Beagle" and I heard Lisa say her own name: "Lisa." I also remember hugging her, feeling her arms, etc. It was so nice. Then I am in a car with Zoe Jean and we are going to pick up Lisa, we see her walking on the side of the road coming towards us.

In this dream I saw the man across the street, the son of the old lady who lives there and she is weird too. In the dream he was playing music on his front lawn, like a band but by himself. Then Zoe Jean Jean, Greg and me all got involved in it. In the dream he wasn't so weird as he is in real life.

Cannot remember much in this dream but before I woke up I was dreaming. Me and someone else was at a store at the Cape. I went to go in, but it was not opened yet. I think Greg was inside as he worked there, but I had my own shop a few stores down. I remember wanting to go to the other end of the bay, but along the waterfront. So I was cutting through people's yards, at one yard I had to go around as their building stuck out into the water. When I was doing so, I saw some dogs in front and I ran back to the tree, they saw me and came after me, but were friendly. I was still trying to get across and I woke up.

I was taking a shower and I remembered part of a dream I had the night before, I was at Destiny's and she was home and she said her and her boyfriend just got out of jail. They got arrested for fighting.

Cow Dream I was a cow in this dream and for some reason all the cows were chasing me. I somehow got on the edge of the grain silo, named after my grandmother Maiden name. Some people call it The Flying Cows.

Last night I had a cat dream, (we lost Angel our beloved cat on Sat.) I cannot remember the whole dream, but it was of a white cat and she lived somewhere nice but left and arrived in a strange land. I saw her riding on the door handle of a car and then she jumped off into a field. In my dream, she was a young cat. After she was in the field, she saw a house and the children that lived there saw her and I would say three or four children, in sort of old country style clothes, long skirts, kerchiefs on their heads. They were all so happy and smiling to see this beautiful white cat. The cat crossed the road to them and they brought her inside to meet their mother. She was very glad to see this beautiful special cat. I think the dream was sent to me, maybe by Angel, to show me she is fine and young and happy in her new home. :-) Our wonderful animal companions, our family. It's so hard to lose them, but we are blessed with their love always. Angel was the most loving cat I have ever known, so full of love and she took care of the young Siamese kittens, like they were her own. I will always love her and never forget her beautiful eyes and the way she would look at you as she crawled up beside you. Her eyes would be saying, "is it ok?" And you would pat her and she would stare at you with so much love.

I did not write down my dream in time to remember it, but I did have a dream with my brother, Dickie in it. It was nice to see him. :-)

Bad dream and I don't know where it came from. Like a horror movie, and I have not watched or read anything like it. It was at a hotel, I was there and I had a little boy. Some guy broke in and wanted to hurt him, or something to that effect. I called the police. Then some other man tried to help, and there was a big fight. I was hiding in the room and another girl with me. The fight ended up in the bathroom. Then the bad guy brought out the man helping, and his head was taped to a container with the opening going into his mouth so that whatever was poured into it the man had to swallow. And his hands were bound. Then I woke up. It was crazy.

I was in a house that was mine but the cellar was different. Some friends were over and they stayed overnight during the Christmas holidays. We all made apple turnovers and I had some extra dough and gave its to Zoe Jean to play with outside. In the cellar I found this sticky stuff on the wall, it looked like saddle soap, I showed everyone and we figured it was this glue stuff like the oil man leaves for the furnace. Then Joey and his friend were shutting off the electric to fix some wires. I woke up but the dream seemed so real.

The Alligator Dream In this dream I was driving my car and I got some guy really pissed off at me. I do not know why. I stopped my car and ran down a hill into a lake. I thought I was safe and I flipped him off. At that moment an alligator grabbed me and ate me. I remember in the dream thinking so this is what it is like to be eaten by an alligator. It was not a pleasant thing to experience.

Last night I dreamed Lisa Jean was with me, and she was driving my Volkswagon bug, there was snow on the ground. We were at a restaurant with some kids, not sure who the little kids were. Lisa Jean was younger, her hair and face looked more like when she was little, shorter hair, curly but as we were walking to the the car she was talking and she reminded me of the girl who works at Stop and Shop. That girl reminds me of Lisa Jean but the weird part was Lisa said to me, I know I remind you of Samatha. I don't know how Lisa knew of her, so I did not say anything. Then Lisa drove the car and the snow was deep, we sort of got stuck. Then we went to another restaurant and the kids went right up and sat at the bar. I said they could not sit at the bar. The we left and came home. When I woke up, I remembered when I went to the psychic after Lisa died, she mentioned a girls name, I wonder if it was Samatha. I am going to find that book I wrote it in.

In another dream after we lost Lisa Jean, I was trying to find her, I was driving to Franklin and I was calling her friends on the phone asking if they knew where she was. One person told me where and I went to that place. I went into a house and Lisa Jean was sleeping. I woke her up and hugged her. She did not know about anything that had happened. I started to tell her about her daughter and what was going on.

In a dream I was laying in bed and I could see myself laying on the sheet. I was surrounded with these symbols drawn in purple all around my body. The symbols were like swirls in a circle that came to a point. Then the next night I woke up to a sound that was nothing like I have ever heard before. It was a voice sound but not words like oooh but not a human sound. To me it was supernatural. I just laid there awake not moving hoping to hear it again.

Well those are some of my dreams, if you want to remember your dreams you should keep a journal near your bed, and as soon as you wake up from it, write down everything that you can. If you do not do this you will not remember them later on. So many times I have had dreams that were awesome, and I would think, I won't forget this one, and sure enough later on, I cannot remember all of it.

The Vision of Mars

Years ago when I was around seventeen, I had a dream that there was a crash behind a store in the town I lived in. In the dream I crashed there and I crawled out of the crash site and sat on the edge looking down. Everyone died in it except for myself. I did a painting of it, and it shows me sitting at the edge with grave sites next to me.

Then about twenty years later I was working in my garden, and I found this red colored rock, it was shaped like what we think of as a UFO. I thought it was interesting and I took a break and went in and sat down on my sunporch to look at it. While I was holding it, the vision happened. I felt this terrible sadness come over myself, it was so intense that I was weeping. I could see the crafts leaving the planet and everyone that was left was going to die, because the planet was being destroyed or something terrible was happening. It took me years before I was able to paint the vision as best I could.

Years later I took the classes about Project Earth, at one class Nancy was talking about how Mars was hit by an astroid, or something like that, and caused the planet to lose its oxygen. At that moment it all connected and made sense. The two dreams were connected. I have always thought that my spirt came from another planet, and I have no clue as to what happened after that.

Conclusion:

After reading all of my dreams and goals that I had written about in the past, I can now look back and see what some of desires and goals were. I am truly happy with the person I am today, and the goals I have accomplished and the things I have been able to do and the projects I am working on now in my life. I have a wonderful family and support from them in all the things I do. I also have the support from all of my business clients and friends like Evanne, they are there for me at any time. I am happy with the books I have been able to write. I know some are not perfect, or just the way I would want them if I wrote them again today. I feel even though the pictures in the "Change The World Cookbook" are not great, I think what is said in the words and the message is what is important. I know a recipe or two might be missing an ingredient like sugar or salt. So if you happen to get the cookbook and have any questions please feel free to email me. I am still working on my goals of being a better vegetarian, I was a serious one for years and slowly slipped back to the meat and veggie diet. So I am more like that person who eats a lot less meat, but I still eat some. So my new goal is to really get going on cooking more veggie meals. I appreciate all the help I get with my books from the artists who donate their work. I hope people see it and reach out to them for drawings. I am sure they are capable of fulfilling any art project your interested in. Reach out to me if you would like contact any artist you have seen in any of my books. This is the conclusion of my book and the things I have written about through the years. I have much more to contribute so maybe there will be a book two sometime in the future. I know I would like to put all of my art into one book. Please let me now what you thought, or if you have any questions. I can be reached at zling13@comcast.net. Much Love, Stardragon.

The End:

Other books you will also enjoy:

Duck and Spider

Tabitha

The Tabitha Tree

Secret Friends

Henry and Sara

Change the World Cookbook

Skye

Dinner at Dragons House

Build Your Own Squirrel Proof Bird Feeder

What It Was Like When I Was Little

Dragon Eyes

The Great Cooking Contest

The King's Journey

Retrospective Zoe Jean

Are You A Hoarder?

Two Hungry Bears

The Flower That Wanted To Dance

Dragon Art From The Dungeons Across America

Within The Gates Of Hell: True Covid-19 Stories by Inmates

Thank you, I hope you enjoyed my journey. May The Dragons Fire Light Your Way-One Love, Stardragon.

The Artist: MR. Eddie King: His art came to me at the perfect time, I had no idea what I wanted for the cover and then this wonderful person just sends me some of his art out of the blue. I took one look at it and said to myself, this might be just the right picture for my cover.

The Artist: My name is Eddie King and I'm a 56 year old black artist. I was raised in Kalamazoo, Michigan and decided to set out on my own journey of self-discovery at the age of fifteen. Aimlessly headed to no-where and I got involved with the gang lifestyle which has led me to various jails and prisons incarcerations. Up to the age 39 my life was routine, locked up for a few years to get out for a few months and back in. So in 2007 I was charged with six armed robberies and one endangering safety and I pleaded out to do thirty years inside the Wisconsin prison system. I don't blame anyone but myself for my irrational thinking. So I am 100% guilty for my actions, and I came to realize that if I don't want to die inside prison then I need to change my ways. I've studied many religious teachings and no religious books, Judaism, Christianity, or Moslem didn't give me peace of mind, so I started to doodle to free my mind. For the last twelve years I advance from drawing stick figures to painting portraits. I have had no formal art schooling besides reading a few art book. Now my present and future life is centered around finding other artists and making a future of being a professional artist. I am seeking out an art sponsor and any education/knowledge that will assist me on my journey.

All Rights reserved. No part of this book may be reproduced, stored in. Retrieval system or transmitted in any form or by any means without prior written permission of the author, except by a reviewer who may quote brief passages in a review to be printed in a newspaper, magazine or journal.

Made in the USA
Columbia, SC
25 July 2024

c612ff15-1817-4798-bdd0-73b4614aed2eR01